THE CA[obscured]
(Fren[obscured]

Off the Australian coas[obscured] commander of the British steamer *Georgette* hailed the American whaler *Catalpa*.

'You have six convict prisoners on board. I give you fifteen minutes to consider, . . . and if you don't heave to I'll blow the masts out of you.'

Pointing to the Stars and Stripes, Captain Anthony of the *Catalpa* replied with classic brevity.

'That's the American flag. I am on the high seas. If you fire on this ship, you fire on the American flag.'

That was the dramatic climax to the incredible story of one of the most daring and skilfully planned rescues ever effected. it began in 1866 when the British authorities discovering that more than a third of the regular troops of the British Army in Ireland were Fenians, arrested and courtmartialled large numbers, some of whom were deported to Western Australia. The general amnesty of 1871 did not apply to a small number of prisoners under sentence of penal servitude in Fremantle. They felt forgotton and forsaken. But John Devoy took up their cause. In 1874, he persuaded the annual convention of Clan na Gael in Baltimore in the United States to organize a rescue plan. Funds were raised and a whaling bark bought and fitted out. This was the famous *Catalpa*, which, under the command of Captain George S. Anthony of New Bedford set out for Australia on 29 April 1875 . . .

Cover illustration by Terry Myler

SEÁN Ó LÚING

FREMANTLE MISSION

ANVIL BOOKS

Anvil Books Ltd., Tralee, County Kerry
Republic of Ireland, 1965

Made and printed in the Republic of Ireland
by Browne and Nolan Limited, The Richview Press, Dublin
Set in Linotype Times
Cover design by Joe O'Byrne, M.I.A.P.I.

It is well to love liberty, for it demands much of those who would live by it. Liberty is not content to share mankind. John Boyle O'Reilly, who came to Boston by way of a penal colony in Western Australia, understood this as few men have. "Freedom," he wrote, "is more than a resolution— he is not free who is free alone."

To those who in our time have lost their freedom, or who through the ages have never won it, there is a converse to this message. No one—in the darkest cell, the remotest prison, under the most unyielding tyranny—is ever entirely lost in bondage while there are yet free men in the world. As this be our faith, let it be also our pride.

—St. Patrick's Day greeting from
President Kennedy.
Wexford People, Saturday, 31 March 1962.

DOM DHEARTHÁIR
DÍLIS PÁDRAIG

CONTENTS

CONTENTS—*Continued.*

ACKNOWLEDGMENTS

The author wishes to acknowledge his appreciation of the help received from the courteous and efficient staffs of the National Library and the State Paper Office while engaged in research for this volume.

CHAPTER ONE

THE HOUSE IN CLARE LANE

CLARE LANE is a little cul-de-sac off Clare Street, not far from Merrion Square, in the city of Dublin. Number one Clare Lane is still standing, little different on the outside from what it was in the year 1865, when Peter Curran, vintner, as he is described in the contemporary *Thom's Directory*, kept his licensed premises there. The little building is mellowed with age, and has gone a trifle shabby, but it still has the look of a public house, with its large bar window on the ground floor. Tucked half-privately behind the tall Georgian houses of the neighbourhood, its secluded position was an invitation to anybody who liked a cosy tavern and a discreet drink.

To this house came John Devoy many times during the latter half of 1865 and beginning of 1866. On the evening of 17 January 1866 he brought with him a remarkable companion, one John McCafferty, of Sandusky, Ohio, who had been a cavalry officer in the Confederate army. A man of few words and of cold manner, he had seen a great deal of active service in the American Civil War as an officer of Morgan's Guerillas and had proved his courage in many daring exploits. Neither he nor Devoy were drinking men and their business in Peter Curran's house was not to clink glasses.

Peter Curran was a "friend." That meant to those who were aware of its significance that he was a sworn member of the I.R.B., the Irish Republican (or Revolutionary) Brotherhood, also known as the Fenian Brotherhood or organisation. Devoy was 23 years of age, of dark complexion, solid, stocky build, and the iron-firm set of his jaws showed great force of character. Since his return in 1862 from Algeria, where he had served in the French Foreign Legion, he had been made the Fenian centre or organiser for the part of County Kildare which included Naas, Kilcullen, his native parish of Kill and the Bog of Allen. In October 1865 he became, what he was now, the Chief Organiser of the Irish Republican Brotherhood in the British army.

Also to Peter Curran's house there came at intervals certain men who wore the uniform of the British army. They drank little and they used to meet, not in the public bar downstairs, but in the private parlour overhead. They had come there on John Devoy's orders the evening he was accompanied by McCafferty. They were all cavalrymen and their group was made up of about twelve of the Fifth Dragoon Guards and of as many more from the Tenth Hussars.

The man Devoy introduced to them was no ordinary person. McCafferty's reputation among his American colleagues stood high and Colonel Tom Kelly, who knew him well, had told Devoy many stories of his prowess. For instance, how he had taken a detachment of his men behind the Union lines, captured a lot of ammunition, loaded it on barges which he had seized and brought his booty down the Mississippi, raked by fire from Federal batteries. Devoy had related these stories to the Fenian cavalrymen and told them McCafferty was to be their commander in the coming rising, or at any rate that he would select some of their number for special service.

So it was with no little interest that they watched him and listened to him. Physically and mentally they were splendid types, fully trained in the traditional way of cavalry tactics, the headlong charge with sword or lance. They were eager to hear what McCafferty had to say about cavalry warfare, because they had admired his exploits and knew he had been selected to lead them in the Fenian insurrection. His concept of cavalry warfare was new and surprising. McCafferty's battle experience in the American Civil War had been with irregular cavalry, which used to engage in swift raids and sudden forays, but never charged in the regular manner. They only fought at close quarters when necessary and mainly used revolvers with telling effect. This was fighting quite unlike what the British army men had been trained to, and they were disappointed at McCafferty's address. John McCafferty was brief and to the point. He told them in his cold, quiet, efficient manner what could be done by way of cavalry action in an Irish rising. His turns of speech were strange to them.

"I believe in a partisan warfare," he said, but only a very few of those present knew that partisan meant "guerilla." He went on to describe the kind of action he expected and it did not include sword-fighting to which the men had been trained. "Would you not use swords at all, sir?" asked Martin Hogan quietly. Nothing but revolvers, said McCafferty. They were all expert swordsmen. Martin Hogan of the Fifth Dragoon Guards was one of the best and strongest sword fighters in the British army. He had cut in two an iron bar hanging from a barrack room ceiling with one mighty cleave of his sabre. Naturally the men were disappointed when McCafferty said this. Their experience had not included revolver fighting.

Before the conference was over, however, they began to understand McCafferty better. After all, he had seen four years' continuous action and he should know what he was talking about. Whether McCafferty could adapt the American guerilla cavalry methods to Irish conditions was a question which was debated but never put to the test. The territory where McCafferty fought was only thinly settled, with wide spaces and vast distances, and Irish terrain was very different. He would probably have to change his ideas when it came to actual fighting. His Southern States accent and ways of speech sounded strange to his listeners and left them slightly puzzled at times. They might not find it easy to get used to him.

Devoy, listening attentively, saw all this and sized up the situation. He knew, however, that there were many other American cavalry officers of experience in the Fenian organisation who were expected to take commands in the Irish uprising. There was Colonel Kerwin of Wexford, whose campaigning with the army of the Potomac was of a kind more like European methods of warfare. There was Tipperaryman Captain Joseph Carroll of the Fifth New York Cavalry, who had served under General Phil Sheridan in his Shenandoah Valley campaign and in the pursuit of Lee's army up to

Appomatox, had been wounded at the battle of Winchester, and could fight on horseback or on foot, as occasion demanded. These were Irish born and the men would be more at home with them. But there was no denying McCafferty's determination and ability, and his brief, cold, decisive manner, even if it did not win the men's affection, impressed them with a sense of his ability and resolution.

The men to be placed at his disposal were of the finest calibre. They evoked the admiration of John Devoy, who was not easy to please when it came to assessing men. Besides the sword-fighting expert, Martin Hogan, the company included James Wilson, intellectually one of the best men in the army, Patrick Keating and the dashing, knightly, poetic John Boyle O'Reilly.

This was no isolated gathering of a small group of British army Fenians, nor was Peter Curran's house the only rendezvous of this kind. In this year of 1865 the British army quartered in Ireland was permeated through and through with Fenianism and its character as a British army could be truly said not to exist. Had they known the real state of affairs, the administrators of Irish government would have been struck dumb with horror. There were eight thousand sworn Fenians in the regiments stationed in Ireland.

"The Currans of Clare Lane" was a byword among the Fenians of Dublin. Peter Curran had come to Dublin as a mere boy from Killucan, County Westmeath, where he was born about 1841, and had started early in business. His house became the rendezvous for some of the most daring spirits of the I.R.B. and a noted centre of hospitality to men in the republican cause. Many of the north of England I.R.B., over in Dublin for the projected Fenian rising, were kindly received and lodged at Curran's when food ran out and cash failed. To Curran's house used to come Colonel Kelly, Captain Deasy, John Nolan who organised the Ulster I.R.B., Captain Larry O'Brien, Tom Costello and nearly all the Dublin leaders. But it was, foremost of all, the favourite meeting place of the leading I.R.B. men of the British regiments stationed in Dublin.

Gatherings of soldier Fenians took place in other taverns besides Curran's. They were normally casual affairs, not organised meetings like the one called for the McCafferty interview. The soldier Fenians met in Hoey's public house, or the room over it, in Bridgefoot Street, not far from the Royal barracks. This house does not now exist, and all the Bridgefoot Street of those Fenian days is cleared away. The bartender, a man named Furey, was in the I.R.B. They met also at Pilsworth's in James's Street, Fortune's in Golden Lane, Doyle's tavern nearby, Bergin's in James's Street, Barclay's in the same street, "The Bleeding Horse" in Camden Lane and many others. The meeting in Clare Lane, exclusively of cavalrymen, was only one small item in the vast scheme of organisation of the Irish Republican Brotherhood which threatened to undermine the structure and morale of the British army in Ireland.

It is necessary to give a brief account of the I.R.B. and of the circumstances in which thousands of men wearing the British army uniform became soldiers of the Irish Republican Brotherhood.

CHAPTER TWO

THE IRISH REPUBLICAN BROTHERHOOD

I . . . . do swear allegiance to the Irish Republic, now virtually established; that I will take up arms at a moment's notice to defend its integrity and independence; that I will yield implicit obedience to the commands of my superior officers, and finally I take this oath in the spirit of a true soldier of liberty. So help me God.

—Oath of the I.R.B.

THE Irish Republican Brotherhood was founded by James Stephens in Dublin on St. Patrick's Day, 1858. Its immediate inspiration had come from America, where an active republican group had centred in New York around John O'Mahony and Michael Doheny, both exiles of 1848, and no strangers to the home of revolution, Paris. The movement grew on both sides of the Atlantic and became a vast organisation which eventually extended throughout Ireland, North America, Great Britain, Australia and New Zealand, wherever, in fact, Irishmen had settled. Paris also became an important centre of Fenian activity and communication.

The I.R.B. oath, as given by John Devoy, is set out above. It had variations, but the substance differed little. The oath brought the organisation into conflict with the Catholic Church, which forbade secret oath-bound societies. To the young men this was less of a deterrent than to the older, but various means were devised to overcome the Church's objections and the qualms of the scrupulous. A simple pledge was sometimes substituted for the oath and at least one Fenian leader, John O'Leary, never took the oath at all, though this was not because of scruples. In America the oath was dropped after a time and the Fenian Brotherhood there became an open movement.

Units of the Fenian organisation were called circles. The leader, or centre, of a circle was known as an A. Under him were nine B's or sub-centres, under each B were nine C's and under each C were nine D's. A complete circle therefore numbered 820 men but the rule was never strictly followed. Some circles numbered 1,100, 1,200 or even 2,000, depending on the influence or activity of the centre. An A was considered equal in rank to a colonel, a B to a captain, a C to a sergeant, while the D's constituted the rank and file. The B's or captains usually used pieces of squared paper to keep an account of the numbers enrolled under their command, as a muster roll, to be returned to the A or centre. On this piece of squared paper it was indicated what arms the men possessed. If a man had a rifle, it was denoted with a V; the same symbol inverted, Λ, indicated a gun or pistol; a horizontal stroke, —, denoted a pike, and if a man had no arms it was signified with an O. Only two persons were present when the oath of enlistment was administered, the recruiter and the recruited. Thus no third parties could give evidence of the taking of an oath. A Bible was never used for administering an oath. Its bulk precluded it. A small vest-pocket prayerbook was generally used by Catholic, Protestant, Presbyterian or other.

In time the movement permeated the whole of Ireland, working from Dublin outwards, helped on by the organising tours of James Stephens, Thomas Clarke Luby, Jeremiah O'Donovan Rossa, embracing local patriotic societies like the Phoenix movement in the south-west, or agrarian organisations like the Ribbonmen in the midlands and Connaught. It pervaded public organisations like the St. Patrick's Brotherhood and the National Petition movement. Working through trade and craft unions, it developed into a movement of strong democratic and proletarian character.

A great variety of trades and crafts flourished in Ireland at that time. The Fenian organisation comprised shoemakers, carpenters, stonecutters and stone masons, farm labourers, cabinet makers, drapery assistants, commercial travellers, clerks, national teachers, small farmers, fishermen and railway workers. There was a sprinkling of medical men like Edmund Power, Mark Ryan and Denis Mulcahy. Fairs, races, regattas, patterns, after-Mass gatherings, coursing matches, hurling and cricket games were used as cover for I.R.B. meetings, liaison and recruitment. Railwaymen and commercial travellers carried messages.

John Devoy describes a typical unit of the Fenian organisation. The men in Matt O'Neill's circle, 1,000 strong, in Dublin, were nearly all men employed in the building trades —stonecutters, bricklayers, carpenters, plasterers, with a complement of corn porters and coal porters. Devoy knew practically every one of these men. "I have never seen men of a finer physique," he says. "I have seen the English guards, the crack Highland regiments when the Highlanders were really Gaels, the old Fág-a-Bealachs and the Eighteenth Royal Irish when they were at their best; I have looked at the Constabulary recruits, I have seen the Grenadiers and the Cuirassiers of the Guard in Paris, the Zouaves and the Chasseurs d'Afrique in Algeria, but even allowing for a percentage of small but very sturdy fellows none of these splendid bodies of men were finer than that superb crowd of

Dublin workingmen, recruited from the four corners of Ireland, who formed Matt O'Neill's circle." He adds that their spirit was even better than their physique, as they spent liberally on the movement out of their earnings of (generally) 30/- a week.

It included men of all creeds. Orangemen as well as Ribbonmen enlisted, but no question was ever asked of a man about his religion. James Stephens, the Chief Executive, who had been a participant in the 1848 rising, considered from his own experience that the liberal middle-class and professional leaders of the '48 movement lacked the hard revolutionary initiative, and decided, in organising the I.R.B., to ignore all such cautious elements and spread the message of republican liberty among the plain people of the country.

The popular character of the Fenian movement is asserted by the great O'Donovan Rossa who, in his *United Irishman,* 20 January 1894, writes:

> Humboldt says . . . in a struggle for liberty in oppressed nations, the lower you go among the people the warmer and the truer you will find them to the cause of their native land. So say we in our life-long knowledge of the Irish people in their struggle for freedom.

John O'Leary, editor of the Fenian weekly, *The Irish People,* calls it a movement of the masses, composed of servant boys and farm labourers, shop assistants from

> all possible kinds of shops, from the country shebeen to the monster houses of Dublin, Cork and the other large cities.
>
> (*Recollections,* II, 238).

The *Daily Express,* a Dublin Unionist organ, and therefore hostile to the I.R.B., describes it in terms as uncomplimentary as possible at the crisis of September 1865, when the civilian leaders were arrested:

> It is a movement without any leader of respectability. A merchant clothier, resident in Dame Street, is the man of most note that has yet been apprehended, and he appears to be a prince in this rebellion of tailors. It is, in fact, a thoroughly democratic conception, its simple aim being a distribution of the property now held by the rich amongst

the poor, and the overthrow of all established institutions, whether lay or ecclesiastical.—(30 September 1865).

The merchant clothier referred to was George Hopper, brother-in-law of James Stephens. The last sentence quoted from the *Daily Express* contains a typically untrue piece of propaganda of a kind which was given all possible currency by the enemies of the I.R.B.

James Stephens, when discussing his aim of giving the movement a weekly paper, said:

> The paper shall be called *The Irish People*. The people are in sore need of a paper at once reliable and capable of supplying the knowledge they require so much—a knowledge of their rights and duties—of the dignity and power of labor—of what they are and might and shall become.—(Document in State Paper Office).

A report written on the movement by S. L. Anderson, an official of the Chief Secretary's office, Dublin Castle, states that since 1798 rebellions have gradated into lower and less respectable strata of society and goes on:

> But Fenianism is even lower than Phoenixism. It is perhaps all the more dangerous as most of its members have little else to lose besides their lives, and the teachings of its leaders inculcate the worst form of communism.—*(ibid.)*.

It need hardly be said that the obtuse official mind could find nothing too sinister to believe about the Fenian movement.

"To enroll men . . . to procure arms . . . to drill men" are outlined by Stephens as the first essentials of the movement in a letter to Luby dated 20 September 1864. The organisation was in the first place a military one. The I.R.B. looked to its American counterpart, the Fenian Brotherhood, to supply officers, arms, money and an expeditionary force. In the battles of the American Civil War, Fenian officers and men gained the experience which they hoped to put to use in Ireland. There was constant liaison between the heads of the movement in the two countries. A significant and important example of the co-operation between the Irish and American bodies was shown in the funeral of Terence McManus in

November 1861. McManus was a rebel of 1848 who was exiled and died in California. His body was sent for burial to Ireland and his great funeral through Dublin's streets to Glasnevin cemetery was in effect a demonstration of Fenian strength and discipline. The movement developed rapidly thereafter. Henry O'C. McCarthy, district centre of the Brotherhood for the north-west of the United States, visited Ireland on Fenian business in 1864 and in a report dated 26 July 1864, at Chicago, gives a brief survey of the organisation as he found it in Ireland and elsewhere:

> When in Ireland, I saw many of the men and a large number of the officers of the organisation. Amongst all I found *earnestness,* determination and a growing impatience . . . I met a large number of centers . . . The men are disciplined and in a great degree drilled. The want of military men was felt, a want that is being supplied . . . There were then 60,000 thoroughly organised men . . . They are in the greater part poor men. Some from the middle classes are members . . . When I was in Ireland, about 15,000 men were armed. There were few rifles, a number of fowling pieces, many thousands of pikes. Pikes were being manufactured in Dublin in small quantities and transported to various sections of the country . . . During the past three months the organisation has grown rapidly at home. It is fast extending in England. The Brotherhood of St. Patrick will be entirely absorbed by the close of this year. *The movement is culminating. Another year will bring it to its greatest strength* . . . In the manufacturing districts [of England] the discontent is ripe for a revolt. Revolution in Ireland would render a rupture between the working classes and the oligarchs imminent in England . . . The organisation has extended very generally in all the States. In Ohio, in Pennsylvania, in New York, in Indiana, in Michigan, and especially in the New England States . . . *But a movement for next year is fixed, and in order to have it we must have the means.*
>
> —(*The Irish Republic,* Chicago, 2 November 1867).

This meant that a rising was to take place in 1865.

An evangelistic flavour was given to the movement by the influential *Irish Republic* which, grouping together the fortunes of Ireland and America, stated in a leading article, dated 29 June 1867, headed "Irish Freedom and Southern Slavery," that "The destiny of America was to republicanise the world," and in another leader, same date, that "the influence of ten millions of people of Irish blood and birth, who are citizens and residents of these United States, has yet to be brought to bear on the national mind of America." The paper, edited by Dr. David Bell, onetime Presbyterian minister of Ballybay, County Monaghan, also quoted with approval, 6 July 1867, the views of Horace Greeley's powerful *New York Tribune* that there was now an Irish nation outside of Ireland which was demanding justice for their homeland and must be reckoned with. The proposition that the organisation should invade and occupy Canada and use it as a base for operations against England appealed to a large body of American Fenians, who expected President Johnson to recognise their belligerent rights. Bell expressed the wishes and hopes of these men when he wrote (leading article *Irish Republic*, 29 June 1867): "Possessed of the shores and harbours of the northern provinces we shall proceed to our proper work. The maritime rights of belligerent powers—which England conceded so gladly and so quickly to the late slave-holding Confederacy—will not be denied to us." The Fenian general, Thomas Sweeny, asked pertinently: "Who will say that Andrew Johnson will not recognise the Irish Republic, even if it should be only in name, as long as we have soil that we can claim as our own? It is necessary to have some base, from which we can send out privateers against English commerce." That the Fenian proposition of invading Canada, with overt support from a section of the United States, was not as visionary as it appears, is acknowledged by students of the period (cf. Clyde L. King, *The Fenian Movement*, University of Colorado Studies, April 1909). Men of influence at Washington were planning an invasion of Canada, and Senator Zach Chandler of Michigan worked out a plan which was backed by thirty leading senators. The Fenians actually did invade Canada in 1866 and 1870 on a very limited scale and without success.

A despatch from the British Consul in Philadelphia, dated 5 February 1865, suggests that the organisation was formidable and flourished in the anti-British atmosphere created by Britain's favour towards the Confederate States. The

Consul said that the Brotherhood had its ramifications throughout the United States, Canada and Ireland, was confined principally to the Roman Catholic Irish, but was not generally encouraged by the Catholic clergy. The Roman Catholic clergy of Pennsylvania had been exhorted by their Bishop to preach against it. Hatred of the English government, explained the Consul, was fostered by the Press, by the masses of American population and many of the educated classes. (Document in State Paper Office).

It is not easy to estimate the Fenian strength in the United States, and there is much exaggeration in the figures for Ireland and America given by an informer to the Consul at Philadelphia and sent by him to the Home Office in November 1865. These are:

England . .	7,000
Scotland . .	8,000
Wales . . .	3,000
Ireland . . .	400,000
United States . .	681,000

The figures are accompanied by a lurid and fanciful description of the material destruction planned by the Fenians throughout Great Britain, as well as by a reference to an interesting proposition "that Ireland be annexed to the American republic." The good simple Consul swallowed the lot and wrote very fully that he was satisfied the information was correct. (Document in State Paper Office).

Six hundred and eighty-one thousand is certainly an exaggeration for the United States. John O'Leary, editor of the *Irish People*, well-informed and realistic, states that at the close of the American Civil War there were 200,000 disbanded Irish soldiers, "gasping to be at the throat of England," a not improbable figure.

Stephens gives a total of 80,000 for Great Britain and Ireland, an estimate which Devoy accepts as being probably correct. It does not include the 15,000 Fenians in the British army. This figure is also Stephens's. But the pervasive Fenian idea of national independence found a response in the spirit of three-quarters of the people of Ireland. A letter from Michael MacLaughlin, a correspondent of O'Donovan Rossa's, will give a picture of the spirit and extent of the I.R.B., in 1865, in Scotland where there was a considerable Irish-born population. (The 1861 census places the number at 204,000.) MacLaughlin was a native of Cultimach, County Mayo, who spent six years building up the I.R.B. in the north-west of Ireland and in Scotland. He wrote:

In May, '65, I received a communication that Mr. James Stephens was coming to Scotland, and I was to call a meeting of officers of the I.R.B., as he had important instructions to give them. That was his first and last visit. We met in the house of a friend in Glasgow, and there Mr. Stephens impressed us with the necessity of renewed vigour in filling up the ranks of the soldiers of Ireland, as that year was to be the year of action, and that on no consideration would the struggle for our country's independence be postponed. The brave fellows assembled there that night, taking all they heard for Gospel truth, pledged themselves that nothing would be left undone on their part. And well they kept their word. I travelled as far as Edinburgh with Mr. Stephens. I called a meeting of the officers in Edinburgh, and they received the same instructions as the men in Glasgow. I parted with Mr. Stephens in Edinburgh . . . From May till December, '65, the organisation took new life. The nearer the hour for action came the more vigorous our recruiting sergeants worked . . . One morning in the second week of December, '65, I was working at my bench when a knock came to the door . . . and with a laugh on his face Dan Downing, then of the *Irish People*, stepped into the room. I clasped him by the hand . . . "What news, old boy?" I said. "The hour has come, Mac," said he; "the Military Council has sent me to you, and you are ordered to report in Ireland with your command" . . . He told me it was decided we should be in the field before the first of January, '66, and that I was to divide my command in this way: such of my men as could support themselves till the first of the month should go at once, and they that could not support themselves should wait till the last week; and if some unforeseen accident occurred that prevented me from taking the field on the first of January, my men would be under pay till the fight began. Not doubting the order I received but to explain matters, I started for headquarters in Ireland, met the Military Council, was told to go back to my command and see that the orders were carried out. Back with me to Scotland again. The morning I arrived I gave orders for the officers with their men to report to me that evening for drill and final instructions. I may say that . . . it was the last time I drilled the soldiers of the I.R.B. in Scotland. It was a miserable cold night for the last drill by the banks o' Clyde, but what cared . . . those

reckless hardy sons of the Gael, inured to toil in the coal pits and iron works of Scotland . . . When drill was over, I explained to the men the instructions I received. They were obeyed faithfully. Next day I started down through Scotland; went to Edinburgh, Perth, Dunfermline, Dundee, Blairgavrie, Dalkeith, Coat Bridge, Dumbarton, Port Glasgow and Greenock . . . and other places. If C.K. of Dundee is alive, I wish him to know that he is remembered out here by the shores of the Pacific by his old friend Mac, for he then gallantly responded with his men when duty called him . . . On the Monday following all the iron works from Coat Bridge to Glasgow were at a standstill. Where did the men go that worked the fires? I could tell; they were gone to Ireland.
—(*United Irishman,* New York, 25 February 1888).

Naturally the government had some idea of what was going on. From all parts of Ireland the police sent in reports, which are not always noted for accuracy. A small knot of informers plied their trade but their contribution to the government's knowledge was relatively unimportant. Dublin Castle despatched sub-Inspector Thomas Doyle to New York to keep an eye on Fenian affairs, and he sent back some interesting reports and a lot of press-cuttings. There are bulky archives of American consular reports in London and stacks of police reports in Dublin about the Fenian movement. These, and a great variety of other material, remain to be sifted by historians and evaluated before approximate conclusions can be drawn about the full extent and impact of the I.R.B.

So widespread did the movement become in Ireland that within a few years of its inception, and with the advent of the *Irish People,* it lost the character of a secret society and people became vaguely aware that a great movement was in progress. Amongst the London Irish the movement, though small, was highly efficient. The task of organising the London Irish was given, in 1863, to James J. O'Kelly, later an M.P., and one of the most active and thorough leaders of the movement. Progress in London was slow at first, but by contacts made through social, political and religious organisations an important group of young men was brought together. It included James Clancy and Joseph I. C. Clarke, both of whom were later on the editorial staff of the *New York*

Herald, and other literary men. The movement made no headway among the wealthier Irish classes in England. O'Kelly wrote: "It found its most active workers among artisans and labourers who experienced to the full all the disadvantages of being Irish in their fight for existence in the great city."

A drill hall was established near Burton Crescent, not far from Euston. Here under the guise of maintaining a gymnasium, hundreds of Fenians learned their preliminary military drill. The organisation was slow in spreading. In time twenty centres were appointed. A compact local organisation was maintained, under O'Kelly as Head Centre, until 1864, practically separate from the general Irish organisation. Communication with James Stephens was carried on indirectly, through Devoy, by O'Kelly on behalf of the entire London body. In 1864 O'Kelly joined the French Foreign Legion to perfect his military training, and Stephens abolished the London head centreship, leaving each of the centres there to communicate directly with himself. Without O'Kelly's guiding hand the London body became dislocated, but held together with remarkable tenacity. It was well armed and trained. In 1865 a large number of London men were called to Dublin in expectation of a rising and they came supplied with arms. For weeks they wandered aimlessly around Dublin and at last they returned to London disappointed. This caused demoralisation amongst the London I.R.B. and when O'Kelly returned in 1867 he had to re-organise the whole London body, having resumed the head centreship by wish of the men themselves. O'Kelly bears witness that the London rank and file were utterly dedicated to their purpose.

In the north of England the I.R.B. flourished strongly among the large Irish population which had emigrated to the manufacturing centres in the years following the Great Famine of 1847. Wherever Irishmen centred, the I.R.B. followed and took root. The British army contained great numbers of Irishmen. Some had joined it out of a love of adventure or soldiering, but the great bulk of them had joined it because they could find no other employment. The recognised Irish regiments of the army furnished some of the most valuable material to the I.R.B. and became important centres of Fenianism. John O'Leary spoke the plain truth when he said (*Recollections,* II, 228):

> It was now to be proved beyond dispute that England could not in the least rely upon the Irish soldiers in her army.

This is no overstatement.

CHAPTER THREE

THE SOLDIER FENIANS

THERE were in Ireland in 1865 about 26,000 regular troops of the British army. Of these, 8,000 were sworn members of the I.R.B. Such is the testimony of John Devoy who, from October 1865 to the time of his arrest in February 1866, was chief organiser of the Fenian movement in the British army. In the British regiments stationed outside of Ireland there were 7,000 I.R.B. men. In addition there was the militia in Ireland, numbering about 12,000, of whom more than half had been sworn into the Fenian ranks. But the militia was not under arms because in the circumstances the Government dared not call it out.

As a warlike organisation the first essential of the Fenian movement was fully trained men. In the British army, trained and ready to hand, was an immense pool of desirable military potential. The rank and file of the British regiments was largely Irish. Devoy places the percentage of Irish as high as sixty per cent of the entire army, including those of immediate Irish ancestry born in Great Britain. This, if approximate, was an astonishingly high proportion, but Devoy was not given to exaggeration. A large number of adjutants and non-commissioned officers were Irish as well.

The Fenian movement penetrated into the British army to such effect that a large section of it became devoted and loyal, not to maintaining the interests of her Majesty, Queen Victoria, but to securing the ideal of an Irish republic. Yet the organisation in the British army was begun in a casual and unauthorised way by two young men from west Cork who had been training in the Albert Agricultural School at Glasnevin. Owing to some trouble they had in the school, they left and enlisted in the Twelfth Regiment of Foot. Before enlisting they had been in the I.R.B. Finding that the feeling of many Irishmen in the regiment was akin to their own, they began to swear them into the I.R.B. They soon extended their recruiting activities to the 84th regiment. Devoy and some friends, out for a stroll in the Phoenix Park one Sunday evening, met the two men and in the course of their talk found they were sure they could recruit the vast majority of Irishmen in the British army into the Fenian organisation. On their own initiative they had already sworn in several hundreds.

It was then suggested to James Stephens that the British army could be a valuable recruiting ground. At first he refused to consider it, but was so impressed with the work the two west Cork men had done in that field that his objections were overcome. The forceful arguments of "Pagan" O'Leary, a strong advocate of recruiting in the British army, had a great effect also in bringing Stephens to accept the idea. Stephens thereupon appointed Pagan O'Leary himself Chief Organiser for the British army.

Pagan O'Leary was a remarkable man. Born near Macroom about the mid-1820's, he was studying for the priesthood in an American seminary when the Mexican war began in 1846, and he climbed out over the wall to join a regiment going to the front. In the course of a battle a spent bullet ricochetted off the top of his head and left him quite literally "cracked" for ever after. His real name was Patrick, but he was nicknamed Pagan on account of the extraordinary hotch-potch of private religion which he concocted. He believed in a Tír na nÓg or Land of the Ever Young, inhabited by all the heroes of ancient and modern Ireland, with their wolf-dogs, steeds and retinue, while the villains and wrongdoers of Irish history, all pet aversions of the Pagan's, were rigidly excluded.

But the Pagan had ability. He had a way with soldiers, for

he had been one himself. A rough, sincere, earnest man, he made a direct patriotic appeal to the soldiers on the basis that it was their own cruelly afflicted country alone that was entitled to their military service and to an effort on their part to secure her freedom. He swore in thousands in an irregular, loose, unorganised way. One evening in 1864 he made a mistake on the bridge of Athlone. The soldier he was trying to persuade called a policeman who was standing at the end of the bridge. The Pagan tried to escape by the other end. There was another policeman there.

After the Pagan's arrest, William Roantree of Leixlip, a neighbour and friend of Devoy's, was appointed Chief Organiser for the British army. He had seen service with the American navy and had also fought in Nicaragua under General Walker. Of fine physique and good manners, he was a highly successful organiser and, in contrast to the Pagan, thoroughly methodical. Recruiting amongst the garrisons in Dublin, Cork, Limerick, Waterford, Fermoy, Buttevant, Athlone, Mullingar, Dundalk, Belfast, Derry, Enniskillen and the Curragh Camp, he obtained a great accession of valuable men for the Fenian movement. He appointed one centre in each regiment. Devoy, checking later, found them all to be first-class men.

It was during Roantree's term as organiser that Devoy first came in contact with the organisation in the British army. He had gone with Roantree on several visits to the regiments in Dublin, and had met the Curragh Camp Fenians at the Curragh races. At that venue in June 1865 Devoy was introduced to lots of Fenian soldiers, and heard a group of them on a jaunting car singing "The Rising of the Moon," a well-known rebel song, as it was driven through the streets of the camp, while scores of soldiers all round grinned approval. Of the 3,000 soldiers in the Curragh, 1,200 were sworn Fenians.

Roantree was arrested in the general swoop of 15 September 1865, and by direction of Stephens, he was replaced by John Devoy. At this same time, there was a warrant out for Devoy's arrest and his name was in the *Hue and Cry*. Adroit and resourceful in his movements, Devoy was not hampered by this. The note of appointment from Stephens, dated 26 October 1865, has been preserved and there was a P.S. to it which said: "Be very prudent now. You owe me this, to justify the appointment of so young a man to so responsible a post."

Stephens could not have made a better choice. Devoy, on taking stock of his position, found it was impossible for him personally to visit all the military stations in Ireland, but kept in touch with the country garrisons through competent local men who frequently came up to Dublin to report to Colonel Tom Kelly, Stephens's Chief of Staff. He gave his main attention to Dublin, the Curragh Camp and Athlone. Athlone was an important military centre, with an arsenal of 30,000 rifles and huge stores of military equipment, garrisoned by only 500 infantry of the Fifth Foot, and some artillery men. Two hundred of these were sworn Fenians, the centre being an Armagh man who prepared to participate from the inside in a surprise attack on Athlone.

As the I.R.B. meant to strike its vital blow in Dublin, Colonel Kelly ordered Devoy to concentrate on the organisation there. There was a garrison of 6,000 soldiers in Dublin, and of these 1,600 were I.R.B. men. The crack Fenian regiments, as Devoy called them because of the strength in which the organisation flourished in them, were the Eighth, Twenty-fourth, Sixty-first and Seventy-third Foot, the First Battalion Sixtieth Rifles, the Fifth Dragoon Guards, the Ninth Lancers and the Tenth Hussars. All these were stationed in Dublin. The Seventy-third was supposed to be a Scottish regiment and wore plaid trousers and a Scotch cap, but there were 300 Fenians in it under a centre named Flynn. The kilted Highland regiments also contained a large number of I.R.B. men who had enlisted in Scotland.

Devoy's task was to organise fully and efficiently the men already sworn in, rather than enlist new recruits, but the public trials of the Fenian leaders in the closing months of 1865 stimulated interest among the soldiers, and new recruits were constantly being brought to him for swearing in. He swore in hundreds more during his four months' activity, but his chief attention was given to properly organising the I.R.B. men in the various regiments. Centres had already been appointed for each regiment, except the Tenth Hussars, by Devoy's predecessor. After consulting the centres, Devoy picked a man to take charge of each company of infantry and troop of cavalry, and got the centres to appoint them. After that the Fenians in each company were divided into sections or squads with a man in charge of each. By the end of December 1865, through Devoy's exertions, the organisation of the I.R.B. in the Dublin garrison was in thoroughly good order.

Each group of I.R.B. men in a regiment knew only its immediate superior. There was an unusual degree of *esprit* among the Fenian soldiers and their discipline was admirable. They were the soberest men Devoy ever saw. There was nowhere else for him to meet them except in public houses, and some drink had to be bought as an excuse. Porter only, and very little of that, was drunk. During his four months of incessant activity, visiting public houses nightly, Devoy saw only a bare half-dozen Fenians under the influence of drink. Both soldiers and civilians used to be present in the public houses, but there were no meetings in the regular sense of the word. To an outsider, the whole thing looked casual. While the others sat at a table, intent on their own conversation, Devoy would have a chat with whatever special man he was meeting that evening. When soldiers were brought to him to be sworn in, they were taken out into the yard, or to a private room upstairs (if the house was a Fenian one) and sworn in, never by a fellow soldier, but always by a civilian, in order to minimise the risk for the soldier who had brought the recruit.

In holding these gatherings of soldiers, Devoy avoided the houses used by his predecessors, which were chiefly near the various barracks. He selected houses owned or managed by Fenians and changed them frequently if he thought too much attention was being attracted to them. In discussions with the soldiers, the words "Fenian" "Fenianism" or "society" were never used. The name of Stephens or of any other man in Ireland was never used, but John O'Mahony was often mentioned, because he was in America and was known publicly as the head of the revolutionary organisation. "But," says Devoy (*Recollections*, p. 66), "the plainest language was employed in these conversations about the object of the movement—an insurrection to free Ireland from English rule."

The Eighty-seventh Regiment was stationed in Portsmouth during Devoy's period as Chief Organiser. It was a wholly Irish regiment, and the I.R.B. centre for it was William Curry. There were few men in the movement as thorough and competent. He swore about 200 picked men of the regiment into the organisation, choosing them for their physique and character. He could have sworn in a lot more, but preferred to rely only on the very best.

An advance guard of twenty of these men, led by Curry, came over to Dublin from Portsmouth towards the end of 1865, having become excited at the arrests and trials of the civilian leaders of the I.R.B. They brought assurance that when the word for a rising was given the regiment would seize a steamer and make for the Irish coast. Some of these men had long army service. One of them had eighteen years and in three more would be entitled to a pension. He chose revolution instead. These men had thirty days' furlough each and thirty shillings for thirty days' pay. Out of this they paid ten shillings each for their passage to Dublin. When their furlough expired and they found the rising had been postponed, they decided to remain in Dublin. They were given civilian clothes and 1/6d. a day subsistence money. They stood their ground and were all arrested within the next two months.

Using his furlough as a pass, Curry could enter any military barracks in Dublin. He was an invaluable go-between for Devoy, bringing messages in and out of barracks, arranging meetings and enumerating the I.R.B. strength in the various regiments. The Fenian soldiers were in greatest strength in the Sixty-first Regiment. The personnel of this regiment was generally supposed to be English, but in fact only about a hundred were. All the rest were Irish and contained six hundred Fenians, with Thomas Chambers as centre. A sergeant of engineers named O'Brien, who had been in a Dublin circle, came home on furlough from Woolwich and put before Devoy a highly feasible plan of destroying Woolwich Arsenal, as the work to which he was assigned there gave him an easy opportunity. Stephens rejected the proposition with horror, but Chief of Staff Kelly considered it would be the right thing to do on the eve of a fight. This was exactly what O'Brien had proposed. He was disgusted and muttered about tender-hearted Irishmen who were quite unfit to fight the English, who stopped at nothing.

But the most remarkable man amongst the Fenians in the British army was John Boyle O'Reilly. Born at Dowth Castle, County Meath, in 1844, he emigrated to Preston, Lancashire, where he worked on the Preston *Guardian*, and joined a company of local Volunteers. Returning to Ireland in 1863, he enlisted in Dundalk in the Tenth Hussars. Before enlisting he had joined the Fenian organisation. Devoy first met him in October 1865. Devoy had remarked to Colonel Kelly that the Tenth Hussars, stationed at Island Bridge barracks, was the only regiment on which he could make no impression. The men in it were mainly English, but there were over a hundred Irishmen in it, and it was the champion light cavalry regiment of the British army. It was called the "Prince of Wales's Own" and its commander, Colonel Valentine Baker, had a great reputation. But the statement in the *Dictionary of National Biography* that "he succeeded in developing an extraordinary degree of efficiency in his men" of the Tenth Hussars requires to be qualified to the extent that this did not secure their immunity from Fenianism. Devoy was told by veterinary surgeon Harry Byrne, a Fenian who had much to do with the Tenth, by way of his profession, that John Boyle O'Reilly was his man if he wanted to make progress there. Devoy was introduced to him and stated his purpose, which O'Reilly at once cordially approved. He was an invaluable man to the I.R.B. In a short time he brought eighty of the Tenth Hussars to John Devoy to be sworn into the organisation. O'Reilly divided these into two troops, obtained possession of the keys of an unused postern gate, and had everything ready to take his men, armed and mounted, out of the barracks at a given signal. He made maps of the locality and suggested the most feasible troop movements. He was then only twenty-one. He believed the blow ought to be struck in Dublin where the organisation was strongest. Eager to make the rising a success, he came to meet Devoy every evening he was off duty, to discuss plans and work out details.

The I.R.B. organisation in the British army remained intact and in perfect shape up till the end of February 1866. All contacts between Devoy and the army were being made without a hitch. If the rising had taken place in 1865, as originally planned, or any time up to mid-February 1866, the whole Fenian body in the British army, trained and armed, would have been fully ready, and at the very least would have set the government a formidable task. The insurrection, which was promised by Stephens for 1865 and repeatedly postponed, did not take place until 5 March 1867, and as a military effort it was abortive. Three main reasons may be given for the immediate failure of the Fenian movement. First, the American organisation had divided into two factions, one led by John O'Mahony which favoured sending all available supplies and men to Ireland; the other led nominally by William R. Roberts, which favoured invading Canada and holding it as a base for operations against England. Personal feuds accentuated this division. Arms, money, men and energy were squandered in these futile dissensions. The result was that the great potential of the American movement became almost a total loss to the I.R.B. Second, the government, alerted by the chance discovery of important documents, arrested the most prominent of the I.R.B. civilian leaders in September 1865. Stephens escaped the net but was arrested on 11 November only to make a sensational escape from Richmond jail on the 24th. Third, the repeated postponements of the fight, mainly on the advice of Stephens, and the arrests of a great many officers of the organisation, had a demoralising effect on the civilian side of the movement.

The movement in the army remained in sound condition for some time after the shattering of the civilian section. No soldiers were arrested till February 1866. Only one real informer turned up in the army, a Private Foley of the Fifth Dragoons, who admitted to joining the I.R.B. in order to spy on it. Some other army men, however, were induced to inform by intimidation and subterfuge. Finally the British authorities woke up to the fact that their army was honeycombed with Fenianism, that as far as service in Ireland was concerned, it could not be relied on, and that, in short, it was in a condition highly dangerous to the security of the government. Shocked and alarmed, they sent all the principal Fenian regiments out of Ireland. The regiments had all gone overseas before the abortive and unauthorised rising of 5 March 1867, except the Seventy-third. This was supposed to be a Scottish regiment but it, too, was largely Fenian.

CHAPTER FOUR

ARREST AND SENTENCE

JOHN DEVOY was arrested in Pilsworth's public house in James's Street on 22 February 1866, along with William Curry, Matt O'Neill, Edward Pilsworth St. Clair, Bill Hampson, Stephen O'Kelly and some others, including soldiers and civilians. The arrests were effected by thirty detectives and as many uniformed police, through the treachery of Patrick Foley of the Fifth Dragoons, who was "arrested" along with them. Not until a further escort of thirty military had been called from the Royal barracks were they taken to Chancery Lane station house. The authorities were taking no chances with men whom they considered desperate. The arrest of Devoy was a shattering blow to the organisation in the army and following it disintegration set in rapidly. Arrests of soldiers and civilians were now a daily occurrence.

John Boyle O'Reilly had been arrested a week earlier than Devoy. As he was being led across the barrack square under escort he was met by his commanding officer, Colonel Baker, who, purple with anger, shook his fist in O'Reilly's face and roared: "Damn you, O'Reilly, you have ruined the finest regiment in her Majesty's service." So he had, if we were to take the angry Colonel's point of view.

O'Reilly was tried by courtmartial on 27 June. He was charged for "Having at Dublin, in January 1866, come to the knowledge of an intended mutiny in her Majesty's forces in Ireland, and not giving information of said intended mutiny to his commanding officer." During the course of the trial, Colonel Baker and other officers of the Tenth Hussars testified to his good character in the regiment. His association and friendship with John Devoy featured prominently in the evidence given against him. Now was revealed the base character of the informer, Patrick Foley, who testified against O'Reilly and his colleagues. In order to show how alarming the infiltration of the army appeared to the authorities, the opening statement of Prosecutor Whelan against O'Reilly may be quoted in part:

> The enormity of the offence with which the prisoner is charged is such that it is difficult to find language by which to describe it. It strikes at the root of all military discipline, and . . . would render her Majesty's forces, who ought to be the guardians of our lives and liberty, and the bulwark and protection of the Constitution under which we live, a source of danger to the state and all its loyal citizens and subjects, and her Majesty's faithful subjects would become the prey and victims of military despotism, licentiousness and violence. Our standing army would then be a terror to the throne, a curse, not a blessing, to the community . . .
> —(Roche, *Life, Poems and Speeches of John Boyle O'Reilly*, page 23).

O'Reilly was found guilty on 9 July 1866, and sentenced to death. The sentence was at once commuted to life imprisonment. As a result of an appeal made on his behalf by Adjutant (later Lord Odo) Russell, who had a high opinion of his character, the life sentence was commuted to twenty years' penal servitude. O'Reilly's courtmartial was only one of many. These were held in the Royal barracks, now called by a remarkable process of history, Collins barracks, in memory of the Chairman at a later date of the Supreme Council of the I.R.B. The courtmartials were intended to have an intimidating effect on the military Fenians. This they did not have, but between them and the posting to foreign stations of the best Fenian regiments, the I.R.B. in the army was effectively broken up.

Out of the large number of military Fenians who were arrested and sentenced it is necessary to describe the careers of six particular men. Their types are fairly representative and give a general indication of the sound quality of the many thousands of Fenian personnel in the British army. As well as that, because they figured in the adventure which is the subject of this book, they have acquired a special identity. These were the six men who were rescued from bondage in one of the most daring and spectacular feats in the history of adventure.

Thomas Darragh was born in January 1834 in Broomhall, County Wicklow, where his father was a farmer. By faith a Protestant, like many of the Fenians, he joined the Orange organisation and was a member of Delgany lodge. He enlisted in the Second (Queen's Own) Regiment on 12 November 1852. In 1854 he embarked for South Africa and was stationed at different forts in Kaffir Land till 1859, when he was transferred to China. In all, he served fourteen years in China and Africa, winning a medal and two clasps for bravery. He returned to England in May 1860, joined the I.R.B. and became centre of his regiment. He was arrested at Fleetwood School of Musketry on 22 September 1865. By this time he had attained the rank of sergeant-major and was on the list for promotion. At his courtmartial, which took place in Cork, on 21 February 1866, two charges were preferred against him: first, that of mutinous conduct at Cork on or about April 1865, in that coming to the knowledge of an intended mutiny in her Majesty's forces in Cork barracks, he did not give the information to his commanding officer; second, that he joined a treasonable and seditious society called the Fenian Brotherhood which had for object the levying of war against the Queen and the subverting of the government of the country. Sergeant Darragh was sentenced to death, but this was commuted to life imprisonment.

Thomas Henry Hassett was born in Doneraile, County Cork, on 12 December 1841. He was a carpenter by trade. In 1859 he joined the Phoenix Society, which was incorporated with the Fenian organisation, and later, after joining the Papal Brigade, saw active service in Italy. On his return he enlisted in the Twenty-fourth Foot, in 1861, and joined the I.R.B. in 1864, becoming centre for his regiment. He swore 270 men of the regiment into the I.R.B. and outlined a plan to capture the Pigeon House fort which commanded the entrance to Dublin bay and contained 25,000 stand of arms. Of a guard placed on this fort when it was supposed to be in danger, sixty men out of ninety were believed to be Fenians. Hassett was on sentry duty at the Royal Hospital, Kilmainham, on a night in January 1866 when he was told by his colleague, William Foley, that a guard had arrived at the picket room to place him under arrest as soon as he left his post. He made his decision promptly. It is best told, with a smart dash of colour, in the words of John Boyle O'Reilly, his comrade in Fenianism:

> Private Hassett walked off his post and, shouldering his rifle, proceeded confidently through the streets of Dublin, in which a soldier with arms is never questioned. It was ten o'clock at night, and it so happened that Hassett knew of a certain meeting of organisers and other "boys on their keepin," which was being held that evening. Thither he went, his steps reached the house and, knowing how it was done, gained admission. The rebels sat in council upstairs: faces grew dark, teeth were set close, and revolvers grasped when they heard the steady tramp on the stairs, and the "ground arms" at their door. A moment after, the door opened and the man in scarlet walked into the room—all there knew him well. With full equipment, knapsack, rifle and bayonet, and sixty rounds of ammunition, Hassett had deserted from his post, and walked straight into the ranks of rebellion. He was quickly divested of his military accoutrements; scouts went out to a neighbouring clothing store, and soon returned with every requisite for a full-fledged "civilian." The red coat was voted to the fire, and the belt and arms were stored away with a religious hope in the coming fight for an Irish Republic. The next evening one more was added to the group of strangely dressed men

who smoked and drank their "pots o' porter" in a certain house in Thomas Street. The newcomer was closely shaven and had the appearance of a muscular Methodist minister. The men there were all deserters, and the last arrival was Hassett. Vainly watching for the coming fight, the poor fellows lived in mysterious misery for several weeks. It is hard to realise here now the feeling that was rife in Dublin then. At least one of the deserters was recognised in the streets by the military informer—Private Foley of the Fifth Dragoons—tracked to the rendezvous, surrounded by the police, and every one captured. —(Roche, *Life, Poems and Speeches of John Boyle O'Reilly*, pp. 124-5).

John Devoy was present at the Fenian rendezvous when Hassett marched in, and it was he whom the Fenian soldier greeted with the words: "Most of those who desert for Ireland's sake come to you empty-handed, but here am I ready for work." His arrest took place on 28 February. At his courtmartial he defiantly avowed his republican aims. His death sentence was commuted to life imprisonment.

Michael Harrington was born in Macroom, County Cork, in May 1825. He enlisted in the Sixty-first Regiment on 18 November 1844, left Cork for Calcutta in June 1845, arriving there in October, and was stationed at several places in India until the opening of the Punjab campaign in 1848. He fought in practically every action of this campaign, winning a medal and two clasps for bravery. Between 1850 and 1857 he took part in many of the fierce battles between the British and the various Indian princes. When the Indian Mutiny broke out, in 1857, he was stationed at Cawnpore. He distinguished himself in the desperate fighting that followed and at the close of it received a medal and a clasp. Leaving India, he landed in Portsmouth in October 1860. He joined the I.R.B. and deserted in January 1866, hoping to take part in the proposed rising. He was arrested in Dublin, on 10 March, for desertion and on suspicion of being a Fenian. After a period of close confinement in Arbour Hill military prison he was identified as a deserter, courtmartialled and sentenced to death. The sentence was commuted to penal servitude for life.

Robert Cranston was born in Stewartstown, County Tyrone, on 18 March 1842. He worked on his father's farm before enlisting, in June 1863, in the Sixty-first Regiment. He was arrested in Dublin, in April 1866, tried by general courtmartial on 18 June and found guilty, on the evidence of informer Talbot and others, of being a Fenian. He was sentenced to death, which sentence was commuted to life penal servitude.

James Wilson was born in Newry, on 6 February 1836. His real name was McNally. The explanation is that it was not uncommon for Irishmen to enter the British army under an assumed name. He served for seven years in the Bombay artillery and left it at the time of the white mutiny, when the East India Company was abolished. He travelled at various times in America, India and Syria. On returning to Ireland he enlisted, in 1860 or 1861, in the Fifth Dragoon Guards, and was sworn into the I.R.B. in 1864. He deserted along with Hogan, in November 1865, when things got too difficult for them in the regiment, where they were continually spreading Fenian principles. Although gazetted as deserters, they remained on in Dublin waiting for the rising and, under the direction of John Devoy, they continued working among the soldiers for the I.R.B. Wilson and Hogan were both asleep when they were overpowered by the police on 10 February 1866. Wilson was courtmartialled on 20 August, found guilty and sentenced to death. The sentence was commuted to penal servitude for life.

These six men were typical members of the Fenian organisation in the British army. As will be noted from their careers they had given meritorious and honourable service, some of them over a long period of years. It cannot therefore be said that their adherence to the Fenian movement was a whim, conceived without serious thought, or out of a sense of grievance, or at dissatisfaction with their lot or any such unworthy or paltry motive. They were young men, but not so young or inexperienced as to be rash. The telling fact is that they joined the Fenian organisation for the patriotic reason of achieving an Irish Republic. They joined a movement to fight the way out of the British Empire. With the decisive mind of the soldier, they went into this project with clear vision and with a full appreciation of the risk. They were only six out of fifteen thousand who did likewise and who considered that the call of loyalty to an Irish ideal was superior to every other consideration. Many of these men had long service and could soon leave the army on pension. They chose instead the perilous way of insurgency, and threw their modest material prospects to the winds.

During the trials of the soldier Fenians there was usually one common factor in the evidence given against them. That was the name of John Devoy and their dealings with him. Evidence was given of their association with him at many meeting places and taverns. Devoy's genius as organiser of Fenianism in the British army was held in respect by the authorities, and because of this the guilt of those found in his company was vastly increased in their eyes. It did not serve to lighten the sentences on the soldier Fenians that their names were linked with his in the daring purpose of the Irish Republican Brotherhood. The soldiers, for their part, looked to him as their leader and guide. He had a responsibility towards them. This was a thought that must have occurred to him often in the dreary years of prison punishment that followed. Devoy, too, had been sentenced to fifteen years' penal servitude, for his part in trying to accomplish an Irish Republic.

Both civilian and military Fenians were sent to serve their sentences in English jails, under conditions of extreme harshness. In October 1867, sixty-eight of them were transferred from their various prisons to the convict establishment at Portland, before being sent out to the penal settlement of Western Australia. Some of them, at least, looked forward with relief to the change, in the hope that they would be under less duress in their new abode. There were fifteen military civilians among the number, including John Boyle O'Reilly and the six men whose careers we have detailed above. The convict ship *Hougoumont,* a prize captured from the French, rode at anchor off Portland, ready to receive its cargo of human beings.

CHAPTER FIVE

DEPORTATION TO FREMANTLE

O God, who art the arbiter of the destiny of nations, and who rulest the world in Thy great wisdom, look down, we beseech Thee, from Thy holy place, on the sufferings of our poor country. Scatter her enemies, O Lord, and confound their evil projects. Hear us, O God, hear the earnest cry of our people, and give them strength and fortitude to dare and suffer in their holy cause. Send her help, O Lord! from Thy holy place. And from Zion protect her. Amen.

—Communal prayer of the Irish exiles on board the convict ship *Hougoumont.*

LINED up on shore, waiting to go on board the *Hougoumont*, were 320 criminal convicts and 63 Fenian political prisoners. John Boyle O'Reilly tells how twenty of the Fenian political prisoners who had only recently come from Ireland were introduced to the hideous experience of being shackled together in double irons and chains. O'Reilly himself, who had been brought there from Dartmoor, was no stranger to it. On each chain were grouped twenty men. The Fenian prisoners were kept apart from the ordinary criminals. Orders to move forward were given, and the forlorn companies of humanity urged themselves ahead to the clanking of their savage fetters. The entire assembly of convicts was paraded, and reviewed before going on board by the prison governor and by the prison and ship's doctors. Then they were formed into columns, still in their chains, and marched to a steamer which was to bring them out to the *Hougoumont*.

A streak of emotion, sudden as lightning, halted the grim advance for a moment. At the gangway, a young girl rushed forward with a piercing cry and threw her arms round one of the Fenian prisoners, sobbing wildly. He was Thomas Dunne and the girl was his sister Bridget. She had come from Dublin to say good-bye to him. He could only stoop his head and kiss her, because his arms were chained down, and she, torn with grief, was dragged away by the officials as he was rudely pushed towards the gangway and on to the steamer. From the deck of the steamer they could see her, still watching them, and his fellow prisoners tried to comfort Dunne with words of sympathy.

The steamer took them out to the *Hougoumont*. Soldiers lined the decks of the vessel. The chains were knocked off and the prisoners told to go below. The 320 criminal convicts were put in the forward hold; the sounds and shrieks and yells from them were like a symphony of hell. The terrible thought occurred to the sensitive O'Reilly, as he stood in the hatchway looking at the unfortunate men glaring from behind their bars, "are my friends in there amongst them?" Hesitating at the door, he was greeted by a friendly voice from a man who stretched out his arms, with the invitation: "Come, we are waiting for you." It was Private Patrick Keating, an old comrade in the Fifth Dragoon Guards. O'Reilly and the Fenian prisoners followed him through the crowd of convicts to a door leading amidships where there were separate quarters for the political offenders.

There were 63 Fenian prisoners altogether. Of these, fifteen were soldier Fenians who were classed as criminals and placed among the convicts. Had the rules been rigidly enforced, their lot aboard ship would have been harsh. It was made easier, however, by the fact that some of the guards on the ship were soldiers who had served in the same regiments as the Fenians. In fact, except for one or two who were surly and hostile, all the guards were friendly to the Fenian soldiers, and they were permitted to pass the days in the company of their fellow Fenians. Only at night had they to retire to the fore part of the ship amongst the convicts. The good-natured guards allowed John Boyle O'Reilly alone to sleep with the civilian prisoners as well, though it was against the rules.

Along with O'Reilly in that group were other noted personalities of the Fenian movement. They included Denis B. Cashman, author-to-be of a *Life of Michael Davitt*; John Edward Kelly, John Flood, Cornelius Dwyer Keane, Thomas McCarthy Fennell, Thomas F. O'Malley Baines, Joseph Noonan, Cornelius O'Mahony and John Kenealy.

There was some literary talent among the Fenians. Father Delaney, the Chaplain, gave them paper and writing materials for a weekly manuscript journal which they called *The Wild Goose,* in echo of the historic and romantic past in which the exiled Wild Geese, after the defeat of James II, took service in the armies of France. D. B. Cashman wrote the title with ornate frills and shamrocks, and contributed articles as well. The editorial duties of this lively journal were shared by John Boyle O'Reilly, John Flood and John Edward Kelly. For others besides the prisoners it shortened the journey. A sergeant in charge of the Fenians spoke of the pleasure it gave him to read the little publication, and tells us it was very popular with all the officers and men on board. He paid tribute to editor John Flood as a gentleman and a scholar. (*United Irishman*—Liverpool—17 June 1876). Seven weekly numbers of *The Wild Goose* appeared, and every Sunday afternoon O'Reilly read it aloud to his comrades as they sat around their berths below decks. Sailing past the Cape of Good Hope, he wrote for it his narrative poem "The Flying Dutchman." Many a year later O'Reilly, then a free man and a leading citizen of Boston, recalled vividly how

> Amid the dim glare of the lamp the men, at night, would group strangely on extemporised seats. The yellow light fell down on the dark forms, throwing a ghastly glare on the pale faces of the men as they listened with blazing eyes to Davis's 'Fontenoy' or the 'Clansmen's Wild Address to Shane's Head.'—(Roche: *Life of John Boyle O'Reilly,* p. 68).

It was a long dreary voyage from Portland around the Cape of Good Hope and across the Indian Ocean to Fremantle, full fourteen thousand miles. "Really I was heartily sick of life on board ship, the journey was so long," wrote Eugene Lombard home to his parents. Half the voyage was done when the idea of *The Wild Goose* struck them. "It was our greatest delight to have a read of it." Yet, he tells us, they lived agreeably; he kept a diary of the voyage himself, so did "Galtee Boy" Casey and others. (*The Irishman,* 4 April 1868).

Tedious as the voyage must have been for the Fenian prisoners, it was nothing short of hell for the mass of criminal humanity stuffed into the forward hold. Some of these defied the harsh rules, and the punishment cell was never without an occupant. The triangle and the lash were brought into use as the instruments of civilisation. From the foremast hung a rope for the final punishment of the hopelessly wicked. It cannot have been a lovely ship to sail in.

Every night the Irish prisoners of all creeds recited together the prayer which heads this chapter. It must have sounded strange within the timbers of that dismal hulk as it lugged its way eastward towards the Australian coast.

CHAPTER SIX

'. . . THE PENALTY OF WHICH IS DEATH'

The sun rose o'er dark Fremantle,
And the sentry stood on the wall;
Above him, with white lines swinging,
The flag-staff, bare and tall:
The flag at its foot—the Mutiny Flag—
Was always fast to the line,
For its sanguine field was a cry of fear,
And the Colony counted an hour a year
In the need of the blood-red sign.—from *The Mutiny of the Chains*, by John Boyle O'Reilly.

THE *Hougoumont* dropped anchor in Fremantle roadstead at three o'clock on the morning of 10 January 1868. Looking towards land, the Fenians could see, on a height behind the town, the great greyish-white stone building which was to be their place of residence. "The Establishment," as it was called locally, was the solitary reason for the existence of Fremantle. The commerce of the little town and the territory around depended on this callous social wart of white stone which marred the natural beauty of the place.

Western Australia was the only one of the seven Australian colonies which had petitioned the Imperial government for convict labour. The semi-stagnant country prospered with their arrival and its economy was largely founded on their work. The first batch of them came to Fremantle in 1850. Fremantle jail, one wing of which was finished in 1855, became the nerve centre of an extensive convict system. The completed job was a large E-shaped three-storey building, surrounded by inner and outer yards, enclosed on the outside by a high wall, and capable of housing a thousand convicts at a time. For some years prior to 1862 its governor was a humane Irishman named Kennedy. He was succeeded by one Dr. John Hampton, who reigned literally with a rod of iron for six years, during which 96 convicts were scourged at the triangles, receiving a total of 6,559 strokes. These are unpleasant statistics.

Barbarian modes of punishment were the rule. Criminals condemned to die were kept loaded with chains right up to the time of execution. Many years later, in more liberal, but for all that, barbarous enough times, Michael Davitt was shown the chain and cat room in Fremantle prison where these regalia of torture were displayed to visitors. Some of the leg and body chains weighed over forty pounds.

The convicts were set to work, under severe rules, in Fremantle, Perth, Guildford, Bunbury, and throughout the interior. They cleared woods, built roads and bridges, and opened communications between one town and another. In Perth they built Government House, the Town Hall, the Supreme Court building and a pensioners' barracks. They built a summer residence for the governor on Rottnest island, off the Fremantle coast, the first bridge over the Swan river at Fremantle, police stations in all the main towns, court-houses, waterworks, jetties, lighthouses, administrative offices and all kinds of public works. They improved the means of communication and administration. Farmers and traders found in them a market for their produce.

During the period 1850-68 a total of 9,668 convicts came to the colony. Their presence gave rise to complex social problems and when they broke the law they suffered dire penalties. In the 1860's the question most often asked in the territory was that of the policeman on patrol after 10 p.m. curfew: "Bond or Free?" Some time prior to the arrival of the *Hougoumont*, the colony had petitioned the British government that further shipments of convicts be stopped. The human cargo that arrived by the *Hougoumont* was, in fact, the last of its kind to be landed in Fremantle. There was a very strong feeling in the town against this last consignment, but it was directed, not so much against the criminal convicts as against the Fenian prisoners who were considered by the loyal people of Fremantle to be more objectionable than the criminals. An Irish prisoner, writing home, says that

> The newspapers in this colony walked into us in a beggarly style before we arrived, but I am glad to see that they have considerably toned down in their views. They are forced to confess that the Fenians are not such a pack of marauding desperadoes as they represented them.—(*The Irishman*, 18 April 1868).

The Fenian and other convicts were taken ashore from the *Hougoumont* in small boats and brought to the Establishment. Patrick Walle wrote home shortly afterwards from Clarence Road, Fremantle, and described their introduction to convict life in the colony:

> Very early on the morning of the 10th we were put on shore in Fremantle, and marched through the little town of that name to our destination, the prison. Here we lay for some two days, going through the ordinary routine of prisoners on the first reception. Dressed in a suit of Drogheda linen, ornamented with a red stripe and black bands, typical of the rank we hold in the colony, to wit, convicts.—(*The Irishman*, 11 April 1868).

The prison rules were read. There was a long list of them and the most frequent and impressive phrase in the recital was, in reference to the punishment for many offences, "—the penalty for which is death." To a free-souled man to be convict-branded and confined in the place itself was death enough. Fremantle prison had its gory history. A mutiny had taken place there in 1857 and the yard ran red with the blood of convicts. The lines at the opening of this chapter are from a poem by O'Reilly on that ghastly, memorable event.

At night the Fenians were packed into their cells, four feet by seven by nine feet high. The place was well guarded. Sentries were posted at the gate and other strategic positions. Their orders included: "Upon no account whatever are any of the prisoners to pass the gate . . . The sentry is to patrol along the front of the prison, constantly watching the prison windows." Should a prisoner try to escape, the sentries were to use every endeavour to prevent them, "but firing is not to be resorted to without the greatest caution." They were to call out "All is well" from eight o'clock p.m. until sunrise, challenge all persons approaching the post between these hours and make prisoners of such as could not give the countersign. "The prison being properly lighted, no excuse whatever will be taken for the escape of a convict out of the prison." The foregoing extracts are from the Fremantle prison rules, dated 12 September 1867. These rules, which were strictly enforced at the beginning of the prisoners' term there, were relaxed to some extent as time went on. But the most effective barrier to escape lay in the character of the country itself. On the landward side there was a vast expanse of bush, an uncharted wilderness, without tracks, food or friendliness, a hostile steppe which wore down the resistance of anyone blind enough to trust to its mercy. For the man who evaded capture, it meant a slow but certain death, for the man who was recaptured from its pitiless wastes it meant the burning slavery of the chain-gang. To seaward there was the vast expanse of the Indian Ocean, which invited no prisoner to escape that way. Or so it was thought. Thus nature was the most powerful jailor that presided over the Imperial Convict Establishment of Fremantle.

Not only that, but the colony was morally and physically isolated even from the rest of Australia. Suspicion was a characteristic bred everywhere within it on account of the presence of the convicts. In the towns all strangers were suspect. There was close surveillance of all ships leaving the colony. Departing tourists found it irksome that they had to accept cards stating that they were not, nor ever had been, convicts at Fremantle. A special force of water police patrolled the bays and harbours. A volunteer force officered by the gentry in each district formed the local defence organisation. There were units of this in Perth, Fremantle, Bunbury, the Vasse and other places. The last of the British regiments left the colony in 1863, and after that the task of defence rested mainly on the military pensioners who had escorted the convicts from England. These were called the Enrolled Pensioner force.

Fremantle was a busy port and a thriving little town in the sixties, with its hotels, shops, eating and boarding houses, billiard rooms, churches and schools. The large white building on the slope behind the town dominated the countryside. In a letter to his wife at 22 Barker Street, Waterford, Denis B. Cashman describes the first days in it of the Fenian convicts:

> We were not asked to work for three days after our arrival, with the exception of pumping some water, the last of those three days being Sunday. We all had the happiness of receiving the Blessed Sacrament, and on Monday morning we were all marched off to the bush to make a road. I handled the pickaxe, dug and broke stones with the boys during this day and part of the next. The soil for some twenty miles inland and along the coast is composed of fine sand which, nevertheless, is very productive. During our two days work in the bush we killed several large reptiles.—(*The Irishman*, 18 April 1868).

Cashman, O'Reilly, Flood and three others were given indoor tasks in the prison for a short period in the beginning while their Fenian colleagues were divided into three groups of about twenty each and sent up country to make roads.

The prisoners' letters home describe their surroundings and reflect their various moods. "By Jove!" writes Cashman to his wife, "won't I know how to perform a bit of household work for you when I get out of jail. Washing, scrubbing, pumping and scouring, with 1,000 other etc.s." Fremantle he judges to have about 1,000 population, Perth 1,600, and the entire colony 20,000, all of which figures were reasonably accurate. The prison discipline was much less strict than in England, while the food was sufficient but coarse. They rose at 4.30 a.m., had breakfast, went to chapel at 6 to hear

Father Lynch read prayers, and, after the day's routine, retired at 9 p.m. The temperature was 120 degrees in the sun, and they had to wear all-linen clothes on account of the heat.

Patrick Walle had a different story to tell. Writing to his father after two weeks he stated that

> the greatest criminals that England ever sent to the shores of this colony are not, nor never were, worked harder than we are working. —(*The Irishman*, 11 April 1868).

He and his colleagues were put at making a road outside the prison; a week later they were put at a similar task out in the bush.

> Well may it be called so, for really it is in a bush we live. On last Saturday evening we were marched five miles, with bed and bedding on our backs, to our rude habitation, which consists of four miserable twig huts and a tent. I sleep with twelve others in the tent.

He goes on to say that at night they were tortured by mosquitoes and fleas. All day they worked hard under a burning sun. Happily they were near the seashore and enjoyed a bathe after the day's labour. There was a fresh water supply nearby also, of which they drank plentifully, as the heat and their rations gave them a great thirst. It was just past midsummer, with the sun excessively hot all day and the evenings cool.

> As far as we can see it is rocky and sandy. We miss the beautiful green fields of the old land, as the appearance of the shrubs and trees are but an apology for the genial smile of our native green. The little town of Fremantle presents to the immigrant eye a rather strange appearance—the houses are constructed in an old fashioned style, of all white sand-stone; nothing is seen but white—white is the prevailing colour; the streets are covered with white sand, which floats about with the wind most abundantly; prison all white, yards white, people dressed in white, but not so with our rations, which are dark and salt enough. In the evening with my companions we arrange ourselves on benches round a camp-fire to hear some song or tale of the old land. So passes the time, just as if we were in as good circumstances as any wealthy freeman. So will it be with us whatever is our lot . . . —(*The Irishman*, 11 April 1868).

Despite their hard lot, there was an affectionate bond of fellowship between the Irish exiles.

> When anything happens to one each person feels, so we cheer, comfort and console each other with a brotherly love.

George Connolly wrote home to his family about his experiences in West Guildford. At first they were to some extent mixed up with those malefactors

> who, I believe, form more than one-half of the population of the colony, and I need scarcely tell you that one's morals are not likely to be improved in such company.—(*The Irishman,* 25 April 1868).

The country around was one mass of forest, with here and there a patch of tillage. Connolly and nineteen other Fenians lived in camp, with huts made of a few withered sticks nailed together and covered with rushes. Each man had a hammock, but neither sheets, bedclothes nor pillows, while a lively multitude of mosquitoes and fleas tortured them at night. They worked at quarrying and blasting stones; they cooked and ate under the broiling sun. Several of them were affected with "moon-blindness," an eye ailment said to be caused by the sudden change from light to darkness, there being no twilight. The letter ends:

> Let not the 14,000 miles which now divide us carry you away to the conclusion that we are separated for ever. No, banish the thought. Seven years is the period of my sentence, and by the law of this colony the commonest malefactor sent from England is entitled to a ticket of leave at the expiration of half his sentence. This privilege, at least, they cannot deny to me. I now conclude by sending to you, my dear wife and children, a husband's and a father's heartfelt love, and remaining until death yours affectionately George Connolly.—(*The Irishman,* 25 April 1868).

Patrick Walle wrote again to his father to say that the work was hard and the fare coarse. He added ominously that though his health was still good he feared, if kept constantly at the present pressure of work, that he would not be able to stand it. Walle was a brickmaker, and thought that if he had his liberty he could do very well at his trade. His eyes were very sore. The country was hard on the eyes, what with looking constantly at white sand-stone, irritation caused by the dust and sand floating in the breeze, the rays of the burning sun and getting cold from being too exposed to the night air.—(*The Irishman,* 30 May 1868).

Eugene Lombard, writing from West Guildford Road station, states that, although not permitted to go more than 200 yards from camp, he was happy and content. He and his fellow prisoners were making a timber road forty feet wide, and were treated in a more kindly manner than in their last station.

> This place that we are in is by appearance very lonely—you would imagine that a civilised man never pressed his foot here; however, there are plenty of parrots and cockatoos, always chattering to each other; huge mahoganies towering to the sky; gum-trees, as thick as grass at home; enough of possums and wallabar (counted game here), and loads of mosquitoes, which almost sting us to death. We manage to keep those away from us by lighting large fires before our tents at night . . . We always try to cheer each other, crack a merry joke, and sing a song of love or war when seated together at our rude camp fire.—(*The Irishman,* 1 August 1868).

A young Irish priest came to say Mass for them and brought them books.

Thomas Fogarty of Tipperary wrote home to his parents to say he had been sick and in hospital, but was now better. His fellow patients were criminal convicts.

> Though very weak and not quite well, I was glad to be released from such companions, and sent back to work with my friends, from whom nothing could be heard offensive to religion or morality.—(*The Irishman,* 8 August 1868)

In another letter home to his father, a Fenian prisoner thanks God he saw but little of Portland prison. His friends who had been there were reduced to skeletons, but their health was improving in Australia and the country was agreeing with them remarkably well.

> You mention also that you will send some papers. You are not aware yet, I see, that I am a prisoner, though working in the country and enjoying a little liberty among the trees and bushes. You must bear in mind that the whole country is a prison, and should you meet anyone they will not speak to you, nor are you supposed to speak to them.—(*The Irishman,* 19 September 1868).

He had discouraging news of Luke and Laurence Fulham, two of his colleagues. They had to stay in Fremantle prison owing to ill-health. Ultimately these two brothers died in bondage.

John Boyle O'Reilly took in Western Australia with a poetic eye and has recorded its harsh traditions and lavish natural beauty in verse which ought to be better known.

In the hard, sad days that there I spent,
My mind absorbed rude pictures.

He had not been serving long as library assistant in Fremantle jail when he was transferred to Bunbury district to work with a gang of criminal convicts. The civilian Fenians were kept apart from the convicts. But it was the common misfortune of the military Fenians that they were made to work along with the crudest types of humanity that the world produced. It did not embitter O'Reilly's generous character.

All around mighty trees, exotic flowers, birds of exquisite colour and strange beasts delighted the eye. By an odd omission of nature, the birds never sang, the trees bore no fruit, and the flowers gave forth no scent. It was a primitive undeveloped country with just such features as it might have had at the world's beginning. The following poem prefaces O'Reilly's collection of Western Australian verse:

Nation of sun and sin,
Thy flowers and crimes are red,
And thy heart is sore within,
While the glory crowns thy head.
Land of the songless birds,
What was thine ancient crime,
Burning through lapse of time
Like a prophet's cursing words?
Aloes and myrrh and tears
Mix in thy bitter wine:
Drink, while the cup is thine,
Drink, for the draught is sign
Of thy reign in the coming years.

In this land the Fenian prisoners bent to their daily tasks, delving in the quarries, shovelling in the roadways, perspiring in the sub-tropical heat. The roadways extended every day further into the bushland but always led back to the Imperial Convict Establishment of Fremantle.

CHAPTER SEVEN

THE CLAN NA GAEL

AT the first convention of the Fenian Brotherhood of America, held in Chicago in November 1863, it was resolved that the organisation should remain in existence until an Irish Republic was achieved. The unauthorised rising of 1867 in Ireland was limited in scale and altogether a fiasco. The main reasons for this have already been given, namely, the split in America and the disorganisation of the I.R.B. in Ireland by frequent postponements and numerous arrests. This did not mean the end of the I.R.B. Far from it. The general fabric of the I.R.B. remained intact. What happened is best put by John Devoy:

> For the first time in Irish history an organised movement for the overthrow of English rule survived defeat in the field. Fenianism promptly re-organised itself and the re-organised movement, while less numerous, was more efficient than that which for ten years had obeyed without question the will of James Stephens. It set to repair the damage wrought by the premature attempt at insurrection and to create a system that would endure, no matter what might happen to the leaders or to the individual men. And without consultation or concert, a similar organisation on practically identical lines took place in America, showing how the race at home and abroad thinks and acts alike in face of similar conditions.—("Fragments of Fenian History" in *Irish Freedom,* August 1913).

The Irish Republican Brotherhood was re-organised at a general convention held about July 1867 in Manchester, England. Instead of the one-man rule practised by James Stephens, the I.R.B. was placed under the control of a supreme council of eleven men, one from each province of Ireland, one each representing Scotland, north of England and south of England, and four to be co-opted by these seven representatives.

Almost simultaneously a new body, with identical aims, was formed in America, but it did not have any communication with the I.R.B. until some time later. This was the Clan na Gael (The Irish Race), also known as the United Brotherhood, and generally referred to in members' correspondence as the U.B., or, following the simple code of substituting for a letter the one following it, the V.C. The name Clan na Gael was adopted on the suggestion of Sam Kavanagh who had been a noted member of the I.R.B. in Dublin. This body was formed at a meeting held on 20 June 1867, the anniversary of Wolfe Tone's birthday, at the house in Hester Street, New York, of Waterford-born James Sheedy. Everyone of the small number present had been in the Fenian organisation at either side of the Atlantic.

The man who inspired that meeting and the movement that grew out of it was Jerome J. Collins, a civil engineer from Dunmanway, County Cork. He had to flee from London in 1866 because a plot to rescue the Fenian prisoners in Pentonville became known to the government. Collins was at that time working for an iron construction firm which had a contract with the prison, and in this way he was able to inspect the building and find out exactly where were the cells of John O'Leary, Charles Kickham, O'Donovan Rossa and other Fenian leaders. Loose talk caused by excessive zeal in seeking recruits for the rescue brought the plot to the knowledge of the authorities, and Collins had to flee to the United States. In New York his restless mind conceived the plan of kidnapping Prince Arthur of Connaught, who was visiting America, and holding him as a hostage for the release of the Fenian prisoners. A house was rented for this purpose. The men he selected for the enterprise belonged to both sections of the divided Fenian organisation. With them was a group of I.R.B. men who had escaped from Ireland to America after the rising of 5 March 1867, and who were then employed by Collins, in his capacity as engineer, in draining the Salt Meadows in Jersey city. The men went down the Hudson in boats to capture Prince Arthur, but missed him owing to an unforeseen accident. The American authorities received warning of the plan, and two of the Fenians connected with it, John Locke and J. J. Finnan, poets no less, spent three days in jail. On their return to the city the group decided to found an organisation which would afford a common meeting ground for men from both factions of the Fenian Brotherhood, an essential condition being that they would have to keep the peace. The organisation was an immediate success in that direction. Before a year was out, John O'Mahony, chief of one section, and William R. Roberts, head of the other, were sitting amicably together at the meetings of the Napper Tandy club in New York. This was the premier club of the Clan na Gael organisation.

The Clan na Gael grew slowly but steadily. It spread over a vast territory, but left great intervening spaces unorganised at first. Branches of the Clan were known as camps or clubs. Each club had a number, given it in the order of its organisation. The first club organised, the Napper Tandy club, in New York, was Number 1. No. 2 was in Jersey city, 3 in Buffalo, 4 in New York, 5 in Boston, 6 in Jersey city, 7 in Leavenworth, Kansas, 8 in New York, 9 in Cleveland, 10 in Cincinnati, 11 in Troy, N.Y., 12 in Albany, 13 in New York, 14 in St. Louis, 15 in Philadelphia, 16 in Chicago, 17 in Hoboken, N.J., and so on. A senior guardian (S.G.) presided over each camp. Besides its number, each branch had a public name, such as the Robert Emmet club, the Speranza literary association, the Wolfe Tone club. An executive controlled the organisation, and associated with the executive was the Revolutionary Directory of Three, which functioned from 1876 on.

The body was extremely cautious in admitting new members, and secrecy was carried, in theory, to absurd lengths. In actual practice, secrecy was never strictly observed. More care was taken to keep undesirable people out than to get suitable people in, and this was one of the reasons why the organisation grew only slowly at first. The Australian rescue, however, proved that the policy of caution was a wise one.

The leaders of the I.R.B. who had been arrested in Ireland in 1865-7 and sentenced to penal servitude for long terms (in the case of O'Donovan Rossa, for life) were released, in January 1871, on condition that they went abroad for the unexpired portion of their sentences. So much did the government respect their influence that it would not let them settle in Ireland. In the circumstances, they naturally went to America. They included Jeremiah O'Donovan Rossa, John Devoy, Charles Underwood O'Connell, William Francis Roantree, John McClure, Edward Pilsworth St. Clair, Patrick Lennon, Thomas Francis Bourke and Thomas Clarke Luby.

When they reached America, the Clan na Gael was nearly four years established. They all joined it. Some of them did not like its over-elaborate initiation ceremonies. Devoy refused to be blindfolded and have his hands tied behind his back in accordance with the ritual, and it was only after great persuasion from some old friends that he submitted. The grotesque ritual was imposed on the organisation by James Sheedy who, for love of the exotic, had joined practically every secret society in America, including the Masons, the Odd Fellows and the Knights of Pythias. But he reserved all his enthusiasm for the Clan na Gael. The pragmatic Jerome Collins disliked the "tomfoolery," and was expelled from the organisation after a quarrel. His later life and death are a part of the history of polar exploration. He joined the ill-fated *Jeanette* expedition under De Long and perished in frozen Siberia. Devoy and other friends kept exerting pressure for years to have the ceremonies abolished or modified, and they finally succeeded, but at the time of the Australian rescue the tomfoolery was in full swing. It should be said, however, that it impressed a good many members.

The Ritual of Initiation contained the words "we are Irishmen, banded together for the purpose of freeing Ireland, and elevating the position of the Irish race. The lamp of the bitter past plainly points out our path, and the first step on the road to Freedom is Secrecy," and the opening words of the obligation which every member had to take ran as follows: "I . . . . do solemnly swear, in the presence of Almighty God, that I will labor, while life is left me, to establish and defend a Republican form of Government in Ireland . . ." A sword figuring in the ceremony was used "to impress upon you that the freedom of Ireland can be secured by force alone, and that our duty is to nerve and strengthen ourselves to wrest by the sword our political rights from England."—(John T. McEnnis: *The Clan na Gael and the Murder of Dr. Cronin*, pages 88-9).

Although there was communication between the Clan na Gael and the I.R.B., it was some years before a formal union with an agreed common policy and scheme of action was achieved. In 1869 John O'Connor Power, who had been a Fenian centre in Bolton, Lancashire, was sent to New York as I.R.B. envoy in order to bring about a union with the Clan na Gael. His mission was not a success because his arrogant manner and excessive demands made agreement impossible. For its second envoy the I.R.B. sent a very competent man, James O'Connor, later M.P. for West Wicklow, and his negotiations were successful. His younger brother, John O'Connor, known in I.R.B. correspondence as "The Doctor" was an altogether remarkable man and became one of the most important personalities in I.R.B. history. Clan na Gael sent him to Ireland in 1872 with funds for the I.R.B. Four years later he went again as Clan Envoy, remained in Ireland and subsequently became secretary of the Supreme Council. He was considered to be the most efficient secretary the Supreme Council ever had. He generally lived in Paris, but his duties called for a lot of travel. A man totally dedicated to furthering the aims of the Irish Republican Brotherhood, he became a Royal Arch Mason in order to cover up his tracks, and this enabled him to travel at will throughout England and Scotland for many years without arousing suspicion. Devoy writes:

During O'Connor's incumbency of the secretaryship, the system of communication between the home organisation and the Clan na Gael became perfect, and the relations most cordial.—(*Gaelic American*, 6 December 1924).

It was during the preparations for the rescue of the six Fenian prisoners from Western Australia in 1875, that the union of the Clan na Gael and I.R.B. was formally brought about, and an event connected with the rescue scheme showed that a close union between them was a matter of extreme urgency. The basis of their united policy is set out clearly in the amended Clan na Gael constitution of 1877. This document defines the objects of the Clan as:

(1) Total separation of Ireland from Great Britain.
(2) The establishment of a republic in Ireland.
(3) To prepare increasingly for an armed insurrection in Ireland.
(4) A declaration of non-interference in [American] politics.
(5) To act in concert with the I.R.B. in Ireland and Great Britain and assist it with money, war material and men.

The 1877 constitution further outlined the policy agreed on between the American and the Irish organisations:

In order to combine the whole Irish revolutionary movement all over the world into one compact federation, acting under a common head, so that it may be capable of acting with vigour and decision against the power of England by securing concert of action and concentration of force between the scattered divisions of the Irish race, the Executive Body is empowered to name three members of the U.B. to act on a Revolutionary Directory in conjunction with three men named by the Supreme Council of the I.R.B. and one by the executive of Australia and New Zealand.—(*The Special Comm. Act*, 1888, *Report of Proc.; Times Reprint*, Vol. IV, page 290).

The further history of Clan na Gael does not concern us for the present. But the foregoing brief sketch of its early years will help to appreciate the problem that faced Sir William Vernon Harcourt when he wrote, some ten years later:

In former Irish rebellions the Irish were in *Ireland*. We could reach their forces, cut off their resources in men and money. And then to subjugate was comparatively easy. Now there is an Irish nation in the United States, equally hostile, with plenty of money, absolutely beyond our reach and yet within ten days sail of our shores.—(A. G. Gardiner, *Sir William Harcourt*, I, 553).

The situation which Harcourt stated in such precise terms was to cause plenty of headaches to successive British administrations. Only in one important respect does his statement need to be corrected. Neither at this nor at any time did the Irish nationalist organisations in America have plenty of money.

It is interesting to note that the Australian and New Zealand branch of the I.R.B. was considered important enough to have one member on the Republican Revolutionary Directory. It was found impossible in practice to fulfil this arrangement owing to difficulties of communication, and it was let lapse. This, however, is anticipating events. The first sensational achievement of the Clan na Gael indicated to the Irish in America the efficiency of the organisation and the competence of its leading personnel. This was the rescue, in preparation over a long period and carried out in 1876, of the military Fenians from their captivity in Fremantle. After the rescue was effected, the Clan na Gael extended its camps into every city, state and territory of the American Union and ultimately became the vast and powerful organisation which backed Parnell and Davitt.

CHAPTER EIGHT

THE VOICE FROM THE TOMB

DURING 1869 and 1870 the movement for an amnesty of the Fenian prisoners grew apace. It was led by three men of ability, John Nolan, George Henry Moore, M.P., father of the novelist George Moore; and Isaac Butt, M.P., and supported by the mass of the people. The large popular vote which returned O'Donovan Rossa as M.P. for Tipperary in 1869 was seen as a tribute to the man and an endorsement of his Fenian principles. The Devon Commission, which had sat in enquiry into the reported ill-treatment of the Fenian prisoners, found that the reports were true and returned a verdict accordingly. The London *Spectator* scarified the penal system which made their ill-treatment possible. The result of the campaign was that all the Fenians who had been jailed following the events of 1865-7 were released, with the condition imposed on the leaders, as noted already, that they must go into exile for the unexpired portion of their sentences.

The general amnesty extended to the men in Fremantle

jail, and the Fenian civilian prisoners were pardoned and set free. Melbourne citizens who sympathised with the released men raised a fund for them. John Kenealy, one of the liberated men, set out for Melbourne but was refused admission to Victoria Province. Anyone who had been a convict in Western Australia was unwelcome on the eastern side of the continent as being unfit to rub shoulders with good Tory society. Kenealy fought his case in the law courts and lost. He returned to Perth to take part in a send-off to the majority of the men who set out in September for eastern Australia. They were denied entry to Adelaide and Melbourne, but the more hospitable city of Sydney took them in. Michael Cody settled in Sydney and so, for the time being, did John Flood and John Edward Kelly. Most of the others, including John Kenealy, went on to America.

There was one group of prisoners who did not benefit by the general amnesty. These were the Fenian military prisoners, the largest group of whom was lodged in Fremantle prison. Despite strong pleas, the Duke of Cambridge, who was Commander-in-Chief of the army, refused clemency to these men on the grounds that if it were granted them discipline in the army would not be the better for it. No appeal could shake the noble duke's decision, and the military prisoners of Fremantle saw their Fenian comrades walk into freedom and suffered the bitter disappointment of being left behind, a small forlorn band of nine or ten men, with life sentences on their record. A great sense of loneliness must have overcome them as presently most of their former fellow-prisoners departed for the eastern colonies. There was an understanding, however, that the released men would effect the rescue of their comrades who were left in jail.

Time passed, and there was no sign of release or rescue. It seemed to the men in Fremantle jail that the outer world had forgotten all about them. Then chance gave them the opportunity of establishing a connecting link with their Fenian brethren in America.

In the year 1871 a public reception was given by the Clan na Gael to the released Fenian prisoners in New York city.

A few months later a newspaper containing a report of the reception found its way into Fremantle prison, where it was eagerly read by the Fenian prisoners. In it was printed the address of Peter Curran in New York and this single item of information gave rise to a remarkable sequence of events. It supplied the first link of communication between Fremantle and New York.

Martin Hogan wrote at once to Peter Curran:

Perth, Western Australia,
May 20th, 1871.

My dear Friend:

In order that you may recollect who it is that addresses you, you will remember on the night of January 17th, 1866, some of the Fifth Dragoon Guards being in the old house in Clare Lane with John Devoy and Captain McCafferty. I am one of that unfortunate band and am now under sentence of life penal servitude in one of the darkest corners of the earth, and as far as we can learn from any small news that chances to reach us, we appear to be forgotten, with no prospect before us but to be left in hopeless slavery to the tender mercies of the Norman wolf.

But, my dear friend, it is not my hard fate I deplore, for I willingly bear it for the cause of dear old Ireland, but I must feel sad at the thought of being forgotten, and neglected by those more fortunate companions in enterprise who have succeeded in eluding the grasp of the oppressor. If I had the means I could get away from here any time. I therefore address you in the hope that you will endeavour to procure and send me pecuniary help for that purpose and I will soon be with you.

Give my love and regards to all old friends—Roantree, Devoy, Burke (General), McCafferty, Captain Holden, O'Donovan Rossa, St. Clair and others, not forgetting yourself and Mrs., and believe me that, even should it be my fate to perish in this villainous dungeon of the world, the last pulse of my heart shall beat "God Save Ireland."

Direct your letter to Rev. Father McCabe, Fremantle. Do not put my name on the outside of the letter.

Yours truly,
Martin J. Hogan.
Erin go bragh!
—(*Gaelic American*, 16 July 1904).

This letter tells us something about the calibre of Martin Hogan as well as showing us the yearning of the Fenian prisoners to escape from their weary thraldom. It duly reached Peter Curran, who handed it to John Devoy. Devoy, even at this early stage of his American career, was beginning to be recognised for his activity and intelligence. He was personally acquainted with the prisoners and felt himself to have a special obligation towards them. They had been convicted mainly on evidence which related to their connection with him and he considered himself bound in honour to make an effort to release them. "I felt," he said, "that I, more than any man then living, ought to do my utmost for these Fenian soldiers."

There was very little he could do at that time, except send an encouraging reply to the men at Fremantle, saying he would begin working on their behalf at once and would let them know further particulars. Then began John Devoy's long-drawn out task of patient, dogged persuasion. He did his best to persuade the Clan na Gael executive that the release of these men was a duty which they must undertake and that a plan of rescue must be worked out. Most Clan na Gael men considered that it was an impossible task and that it would be futile to give it any attention. The faith of one devoted man could do nothing to move them. Devoy was speaking in the wilderness.

The men in Fremantle, waiting and hoping on, were growing more and more impatient under their long ordeal. They awaited the expected letter from Devoy. None came because there was nothing Devoy could do for them.

> Month after month we were waiting with eager eyes and beating hearts the arrival of the mail, expecting to hear from you what we were sure would be glad tidings; but we were doomed to disappointment.

So wrote James Wilson from Fremantle to John Devoy on 4 September 1873. Grievous as had been the disappointment of the soldier Fenians that they had not been included in the amnesty of 1871, many other things had happened since then which galled them as deeply. James Wilson, in his long letter* of 4 September 1873 to Devoy, described them as things "of so base a nature that it would be wrong to hide

* Printed in *Devoy's Post Bag*, II, 562-6.

them." The chief of these was that no effort had been made by the liberated Fremantle men to honour an undertaking made to rescue them. Wilson complained bitterly also that certain financial obligations to the prisoners had not been honoured. Some £500, he said, had been collected in Australia for the benefit of the released civilian Fenians and the still imprisoned military Fenians. Michael Cody came to say good-bye to Wilson before leaving the colony and told him the arrangement was that £64 a man was due to each liberated and each imprisoned Fenian. Joseph Nunan, a Kerry Fenian who had led an attack on Kells coastguard station in the premature Kerry rising of February 1867, was to remain in the colony to arrange for the rescue of the unpardoned men. Nunan and Hugh Brophy went into business as builders and contractors. Brophy had been a contractor in Dublin. An expert workman, he had built a beautiful altar in Portland prison chapel, and was considered so useful a man in Western Australia that he was persuaded to remain there to build a bridge across the Swan river. Nunan and he were in a position to carry out rescue plans without attracting much attention but Nunan, whose special assignment it was to do something about it, did nothing whatever.

One by one the released prisoners left the district. The imprisoned soldiers' anxiety mounted, but Wilson was assured by Jerry O'Donovan that he and his comrades would be got away, and advised that they were not to attempt anything on their own account, but to trust Joe Nunan and wait, that he could not and would not fail to carry out a rescue, and that if any one of them made a move it would spoil all. So runs Wilson's woeful and angry story. Is it true? If it is, then Nunan's behaviour was very odd. He evidently did nothing. One by one the remaining released men left the colony, still re-assuring Wilson that all would be well. Brophy, who had been kind and considerate in every way, left for Melbourne in 1872, and Nunan remained in sole charge of the money collected for the prisoners.

Thomas Hassett now got impatient with the delay. He was working with a road-making gang near Newcastle in the interior of the country, and one day, seizing his chance, made a dash into the bushlands and reached Perth safely. Here he was sheltered by an Irishman for a few days, and with the aid of a modest collection of twenty shillings was enabled to continue on south to the port town of Bunbury, over a hundred miles away. He made it after a journey of great hardship. An Irish family took him in and gave him employment, but because it had been a bad season and poverty was widespread, they were unable to pay him any wages or give him anything for his services but his food and keep.

It was arranged with Nunan that the money due to him should be forwarded to Hassett at Bunbury. A chance of escape soon presented itself. A skipper offered to take him away on payment of thirty pounds. Hassett wrote to Nunan for the money and Nunan sent word he would send it as soon as possible. The money did not come and Hassett pressed Nunan further and sent urgent messages to him through Father McCabe of Bunbury, all without result. The end of it was that the skipper sailed without him. Hassett, now desperate, stowed himself away on another vessel bound for London, but he was discovered on board and made prisoner by the water police which had been specially vigilant since John Boyle O'Reilly's escape in 1869. Hassett's effort was a blind but manly attempt, as O'Reilly said. It failed, and Hassett was for a term with the chain gang.

Other distressing news Wilson had to relate concerned Patrick Keating of the Fifth Dragoon Guards. He had been seriously ill in hospital for eighteen months and was on the point of death when the authorities were prevailed upon to release him on ticket of leave. He left hospital on a cold winter's day, thinly clothed and reduced in strength, and had to be brought back again almost at once. William Foley, another soldier Fenian who used to frequent the meetings in Clare Lane, was unable to leave the district, on being released, because he had no money, and worse still, he practically starved. Wilson blamed the niggardly conduct of Nunan in withholding money that was due to them and thus aggravating their hardships. If Wilson's strictures are true,

Nunan's conduct is hard to explain, in view of his very active and honourable record in Irish Fenianism. We do not know his side of the story and there may be an explanation on his behalf. On the other hand, it must be remembered that their long imprisonment was telling sorely on the Fenians, and the strains and tensions induced by their irksome state of life sometimes forced them to hasty utterances when there may have been less ground for complaint than they thought.

This letter of 4 September 1873 from Wilson to Devoy contains one notable passage. In it Wilson suggested a mode of escape which, apart from some differences in detail, was the one eventually adopted. He wrote:

> There are some good ports where whalers are in the habit of calling . . . it would not be much risk for any vessel, whaler or otherwise, to run in on some pretence or other. And if we had the means of purchasing horses [we] could make through the bush to the coast where the vessel might be and so clear out . . . —(*Devoy's Post Bag*, II, 562).

Wilson was sure there would be no great difficulty in making good their escape, if they had enough money on hand to purchase a passage in some ship. He urged that the sparseness of the colony's population and the relatively small defence and police force were factors which would greatly favour their escape. The total population of the colony he put at twenty-four thousand, scattered over a wide area except for the numbers located in Perth and Fremantle. There was a guard of pensioners, three hundred strong, allotted between these two towns. This, with a few police, formed the entire force of law and order in Western Australia. So he appealed to Devoy:

> Let me tell you that Martin and I expect you to do something for us, we look upon you as our leader and chief, and as such we expect that you will not forget your humble followers but that you will try to get us out of this mare's nest that we have got into. I must tell you that we are much altered in appearance, that from young men we have become old ones, that our hair is now of a nice grey colour, truly if ever we get out, we shall want to make the acquaintance of Madam Rachel. It is now seven years last month since we were tried, a pretty good apprenticeship in the trade of a lag, and yet

you know that John Bull has not succeeded in reforming us. I am afraid he never will . . . Now I hope that on receipt of this you will write in return and let us know what we have to expect.—(*Devoy's Post Bag*, II, 565).

Martin Hogan had also appealed to Ireland for help by letters to his father in Barrington Street, Limerick. This appeal had an interesting sequel, as we shall see. Devoy did not reply to Wilson's letter, because he had nothing encouraging to say. To move the leaders of Clan na Gael to believe that rescue was possible was more than his wholehearted devotion was equal to. So the Fremantle prisoners languished on, their bodies growing weaker and their minds more desperate. Nine weary months and more Wilson, Hogan and other men waited but still no letter came from Devoy nor any sign that help was forthcoming. So James Wilson sat down to write his final appeal to America. Since he had last written, their ailing comrade, Patrick Keating, had been released by the hand of death. The rigour of imprisonment had brought on aneurism of the main artery. Father Burke, the chaplain, had appealed to the governor to allow him out of the prison hospital, where he had spent two years, to a change of scene and diet, and the sight of "friendly faces around him," but he left hospital only to die. He was buried next to the grave of his fellow-Fenians, the brothers Luke and Laurence Fulham.

His death had affected the other men deeply, from grief for a brave and loved comrade and from the fear that a prison death like his must inevitably be theirs too, sooner or later. There were seven of them left. They saw no hope of official release. Their food was neither varied nor ample, and they needed extra nourishment. Doom stared them in the face, death in a felon's dungeon and a grave amongst the convict outcasts of the world. Most of them were beginning to show symptoms of disease, they were all ailing in one degree or another and could not hope to hold out much longer. Therefore Wilson felt it his duty on behalf of all to make one more appeal, and he addressed John Devoy in words that reach across the years with stunning pathos:

I think it my duty to make this appeal to you; my duty to my comrades as well as to myself because no man should surrender himself to death and despair without making some effort to save himself; . . . dear Friend, remember this is a voice from the tomb. For is not this a living tomb? In the tomb it is only a man's body is good for worms but in this living tomb the canker worm of care enters the very soul. Think that we have been nearly nine years in this living tomb since our first arrest and that it is impossible for mind or body to withstand the continual strain that is upon them. One or the other must give way. It is to aid us in this sad strait that I now, in the name of my comrades and myself, ask you to aid us in the manner pointed out . . . —(*Devoy's Post Bag,* II, 566, 568).

This letter was directed to John Devoy, correspondence secretary, Irish Confederation, New York City, U.S. Between these prisoners and Devoy there existed a special bond of sympathy and association, and again Wilson acknowledges their absolute confidence in him. It is a tribute to the impression which Devoy made on them in his role of Fenian organiser.

We expect great aid from yourself who know us perhaps better than any other man in the organisation. We ask you to aid us with your tongue and pen, with your brain and intellect, with your ability and influence, and God will bless your efforts, and we will repay you with all the gratitude of our natures . . . our faith in you is unbounded. We think that if you forsake us then we are friendless indeed.—(*Devoy's Post Bag,* II, 567-8).

As Fenians and rebels they were unrepentant. Their nine years' captivity had not impaired their faith or softened their patriotic resolution. "In the hour of trial we flinched not." Wilson closed his memorable appeal to Devoy by assuring him, no matter whether it succeeded or not,

that the greenest spot in our memory is connected with you, and that we never forget that we are still soldiers of liberty.—(*ibid.,* page 568).

The last words are an echo of their Fenian oath. When John Devoy read this letter he decided that the rescue of these men must be effected regardless of the risks, costs or obstacles. The executive of the Clan na Gael would have to be persuaded, its doubts about the feasibility of rescue removed, and the organisation roused into action. In this grimly cogent mood he set out for the annual convention of the Clan na Gael which, in 1874, was held in Baltimore, Maryland. The Australian letters were in his pocket.

CHAPTER NINE

THE BALTIMORE CONVENTION, 1874

IN 1874 the annual convention of the Clan na Gael organisation was held in Baltimore, Maryland. The proceedings began on 15 July and lasted until late in the night of the 22nd. It was presided over by Jeremiah Kavanagh of Louisville, Kentucky, who in 1861 had spoken the oration at the graveside, in Glasnevin, of Terence Bellew McManus. At this time the organisation had been seven years in existence, but by comparison with the extent to which it afterwards reached it was yet only in its infancy. There were 61 delegates present representing the 86 branches in existence. Membership totalled 6,317. Of these, 4,808 were "in good standing," that is to say, they had paid their dues and fulfilled their other obligations of membership. The organisation included some of the greatest names of Irish America. Besides Devoy, there were Jeremiah O'Donovan Rossa, Thomas Clarke Luby, Thomas Francis Bourke, Captain John McCafferty, William Roantree, Ricard O'Sullivan Burke and many others whose exile from Ireland was decreed in the interests of her Majesty's government. Also present, and prominent, at the Baltimore convention was one of the great priest protagonists in the cause of the Irish Republic, Father Edward Sheehy.

John Devoy's task was to place before the convention the subject of the rescue of the Australian prisoners, persuade those present that it was feasible and obtain their sanction for a plan of rescue. Before the proposition was put to the convention, it was considered at a private conference of five men, of whom he was one, so as to arrange the terms on which it should be put before the meeting. Extreme caution was necessary. Secrecy was absolutely essential, from beginning to end, if the project was to be a success. An unguarded word, a tactless reference, or a slip of the tongue could bring about failure or disaster. Loose and injudicious talkers had to be reckoned with or, worse still, spies and informers. The Fenian movement had already produced James Nagle and John Joseph Corydon of evil memory.

The committee of five, having considered the project, recommended to the convention in guarded language that the rescue should be undertaken. This method of introducing the subject did not work too well. Members were not eager to commit themselves to a nebulous proposition. They wanted to know more precisely what it was all about. It was found necessary to state in plain terms the nature of the undertaking in order to get a favourable vote. This was taking a risk, but there was no other way open.

"I proposed the resolution," said Devoy, "with a full sense of the risk involved in entrusting the knowledge to such a gathering and the necessity of later making it known in a more guarded way to the whole membership of the organisation."—(*Gaelic American,* 23 July 1904).

Not all the 61 delegates present were at first in favour of the project. They had to be given fuller details and such information about conditions in Western Australia as would enable them to judge what the chances of success would be. The policy of taking them into confidence worked. Devoy's incisive and forceful appeal was aided by the wonderful oratory of Thomas F. Bourke and the testimony of William Roantree as to the character of the Fremantle prisoners. The result was that the convention voted unanimously in favour of the enterprise. It was a triumph for John Devoy. It meant that the organisation would raise the funds necessary for carrying out the rescue.

As things stood, there was not one dollar available for such a purpose. Although the Clan na Gael actually had funds amounting to about $42,000, collected during its seven years' existence, this money could not be touched except in the case of an insurrection or a revolution in Ireland. It was for that purpose it had been collected, and the Clan's constitution decreed that it could be used for no other. Each branch of the Clan held its own revolutionary funds in strict custody until such an occasion should arise. Events proved also that there was no traitor or loose talker among the 61 delegates. The personnel of the Clan was well chosen.

Only one of the letters from Western Australia was read to the Baltimore convention. This was Martin Hogan's letter of 20 May 1871. The part of it which referred to Father McCabe of Bunbury was omitted. The report of the convention's proceedings, including Hogan's letter and the resolution to undertake the rescue, was printed and sent out to the 86 existing branches. This report was read, according to procedure, in the presence of the branch members, so that the majority of the 4,808 members in good standing heard it, and those who did not learned that the rescue was to be undertaken. Later on the report was sent out to other branches that were formed after the convention. In the course of the following twelve months the membership of the Clan increased to 7,437, and during this time several circulars were issued to them in which reference was made to the proposed rescue, and a printed copy of James Wilson's letter of 15 June 1874 was sent out as well, in order to allay doubts about the possibility of success. Many members of the Clan queried the genuineness of this Wilson letter. They suspected they were being made the victims of a fraud. Only when the envelope with its Australian postmarks was shown to them were they convinced.

The Baltimore convention entrusted a committee of ten with the duty of organising the rescue. Devoy was made chairman, Patrick Mahon of Rochester, N.Y., with the strong support of Father Sheehy, became treasurer, and Michael W. Leahy of Washington, D.C., secretary. The other members were John W. Goff, New York; James Reynolds, New Haven, Connecticut; Michael C. Boland, Wilmington, Delaware; Jeremiah Kavanagh, Louisville, Kentucky; Thomas Tallon, Omaha, Nebraska; John C. Talbot, San Francisco and Felix Callahan, Montreal, Canada. This number was found to be unwieldy. Callahan, Kavanagh and Tallon were unable to take an active part in the work. Leahy, after a year's activity, dropped away owing to personal misfortunes. The real practical work fell on five men: Devoy, Reynolds, Goff, Talbot and Mahon. We know something of Devoy already. James Reynolds was a brass founder in New Haven, where he did good business. He had a lucid, intelligent mind and, though quiet and reticent, was a very firm and resolute man. From his connection with the enterprise, and his great personal sacrifice for it, he became known as "Catalpa Jim." John C. Talbot was a dry goods merchant in San Francisco and the most prominent and active member of the Clan on the Pacific coast. His ability, sound judgment and application contributed very materially to the success of the enterprise, and since his business interests brought him east often enough to keep in personal contact with the prime organisers of the work, he was in close touch with developments from start to finish. It became his duty to look after important details of the plan on the Pacific coast and he did his work with precision and success. Patrick Mahon of Rochester was a member of an extensive dry goods company. His financial ability marked him out for the post of treasurer, and his business capacity and judgment was an immense help to the accountancy side of the enterprise. Mahon's death in 1880, at the early age of 43, was a serious loss to the Irish-American movement. The drive and energy of John W. Goff was a potent factor in raising funds. He was at this time a clerk in A. T. Stewart's dry goods firm, but was studying law and was soon to be called to the bar. Years later he became Recorder of New York city and figured in a celebrated tribunal which enquired into the bad administration of New York city, carried on, it was alleged, by the powerful Tammany organisation. A forceful, ambitious man, he quarrelled with his colleagues during the preparation for the rescue and took no useful part in the later stages of it. But the addition of Dr. William Carroll of Philadelphia to the working group about the same time more than offset his loss.

Only this group of five or, if we include Dr. Carroll, six, had full knowledge of all the details of preparation and planning. Jim Reynolds and John Devoy did most of the spadework in the beginning. It could hardly be said that anything like a plan had taken shape yet. The only thing of which they could be certain at first was that the enterprise would cost a lot of money and that no effort must be spared in collecting it. It was not yet known how much approximately would be needed. The plan of action would have to be defined.

All they could do in the beginning was to issue an appeal for funds to the organisation. The various branches got busy collecting. The reasons for wanting funds had to be explained, as far as it was safe and practicable, to the branches. Some branches opposed the project altogether, and there were doubts, discussions and not a few quarrels. The only thing that was so far clear and agreed on was that a ship must be sent to Australia. The committee members were not clear whether the ship should be chartered or bought outright, nor had they any notion of the probable cost of the expedition.

The organisation spared no effort to raise funds. Public functions, lectures and entertainments were organised by the clubs and the proceeds flowed into the rescue fund.

John Mitchel could always be relied on to support a project like the present one. As a help towards raising money for it, he gave a lecture in the Cooper Institute, New York. His name was a talisman amongst Irish nationalists throughout the world. His revolutionary writings, his noble bearing during his trial in 1848, his inflexible patriotism, his great book *A Jail Journal* had all combined to make him known and revered. When in July 1874, he was returning to Ireland to contest a parliamentary seat in Cork city, John Devoy was detailed by the editor of the *New York Herald* to cover his departure. At the pier was a group of friends waiting to see John Mitchel off. It was here that Devoy first met Dr. William Carroll.

Dr. Carroll practised medicine in Philadelphia. He was an old friend of Mitchel's. The latter half-jokingly said he wished Dr. Carroll were coming with him. The doctor went to a dry goods store at once, sent a telegram to a medical friend in Philadelphia to look after his practice, bought a ticket on the dock and sailed for Ireland with Mitchel. The doctor was already a member of Clan na Gael, but was not very well known to Devoy and the New York men. This earnest and chivalrous action of his impressed them greatly and was the beginning of a trust in him which was fully repaid by his integrity and practical application to the objects of the organisation. He became a valuable acquisition in the later stages of the rescue preparations. They found out that he was County Donegal by birth, Presbyterian by conscience, had been a surgeon major in the Federal army during the Civil War and had a standing and wide connections which proved to be very useful to the Irish cause in America.

Mitchel was defeated in the Cork city election, which was on a public ballot and restricted franchise. On his return to America, a committee which included Rossa, Devoy and Thomas F. Bourke, went to see him at his home in Brooklyn and asked him to give a lecture at the Cooper Institute in aid of the Australian rescue fund. He readily consented and chose as his subject: "Ireland Revisited." After the lecture, which was a great success, Rossa on behalf of the committee sent him a cheque for $100. He returned it at once with the following letter:

Brooklyn,
8th Dec., 1874.

Dear Friend Rossa,

The good Irishmen who are interesting themselves in a good and sacred work—which I need not more particularly specify— but which calls forth all my sympathies—will certainly allow me to make my humble contribution towards the fund which is to go to that noble use. I think I said to you before, that I could not think of *making profit* of a lecture, the proceeds of which were to be devoted to such a cause. Take back therefore this cheque for $100; I will not have it. When I was in Australian captivity I never could have dreamed of any possibility of escape, but for the means supplied for that purpose by our good countrymen.

Who should sympathise with our countrymen in bondage if I did not?

Therefore, my dear friend, just cancel this cheque; for it would be far more grateful to me—if I were young enough—to take a part in the expedition which, no doubt, will be made, than to derive any sort of personal profit from the devoted zeal of my countrymen in such a cause—which is in fact my own cause.

Very truly your friend,

John Mitchel.

The rescue committee saw at once the value of this letter as an appeal on behalf of the rescue project. As we have said, Mitchel's name was a power. Copies of it were printed and circulated to the branches and it stimulated the collection of funds greatly. The Clan in other cities considered that a lecture by Mitchel would be a good way of raising funds, and invitations began to pour in to him. He would have been physically unable to reply to all of them, but as he was preparing to go to Baltimore in answer to one such appeal, he was invited to Ireland to stand for election in Tipperary. Though far from well, he left at once for Ireland, was triumphantly elected, and died very soon after. When the news of his death reached America, the Clan na Gael, now working incessantly, decided to pay tribute to his memory by a great public demonstration. This was organised at the Hippodrome, where Madison Square Garden is now. The demonstration was a great success and was a significant indication of the strength and efficiency which the Clan na Gael was assuming. It was the first of a series of public functions held by the organisation in order to put its objects before the public.

The dramatist Dion Boucicault contributed $25 to the rescue fund through James J. O'Kelly, who was dramatic critic on the *New York Herald*. Boucicault did not know how exactly the money was to be used for the benefit of the Fenian military prisoners, but knew it was to aid them in some way. Another individual contributor who set an example, at some loss to himself, was the Fenian leader Ricard O'Sullivan Burke who, just arrived in America from Broadmoor prison, was trying to make a new start in life by lecturing on his prison experiences, and gave $75 from the proceeds of his first lecture. It was not the only help he gave, and as a recent prisoner himself, his appeals throughout the States on behalf of the prisoners in Australia were very effective. Devoy did not allow himself a minute's rest.

It was a great help to the committee that they were able to obtain advice from some of the Fenians who had been jailed in Fremantle and were now resident in America. The committee wrote to them and got valuable information and suggestions from them. Thomas McCarthy Fennell, then living in Elmira, John Boyle O'Reilly, editor of the Boston *Pilot*, Denis B. Cashman his assistant, and John Kenealy of Los Angeles all had experience of Fremantle and were well acquainted with the surrounding territory, and their combined knowledge and advice was placed at the committee's disposal. They were able to give details about the prison arrangements, stations, guards, police, ports, shipping and other things necessary to form an exact picture of the situation. John Boyle O'Reilly's advice and suggestions were specially valuable because he had made good his escape from the colony in 1869 and had a clearer conception than any as to what shape the plan should take. It will be seen that his suggestions were accepted as being the most practicable. John B. Walsh of San Francisco was in communication with the Fremantle military prisoners and often got letters from them which he sent on directly to the committee if they contained anything useful.

Nor was it yet clear how many men should be sent out to Australia to effect the rescue or who should be in charge of them. Devoy had set his heart on going himself in command of the operation because the prisoners had been under his charge in Ireland and had been convicted mainly on the evidence of their connection with him. He felt sure that the majority of the committee would approve of his going. For reasons which will be explained, however, he had to remain in America.

Devoy's tentative notion at this early stage of how to effect the rescue is thus stated in his own words:

> My idea was that we should send from twelve to fifteen carefully selected men, fully armed, on a ship calling at an Australian port,

get them ashore in some way unobserved after a man sent by a steamer had perfected his plan of rescue, and take the prisoners off, by main force if necessary.—(*Gaelic American*, 23 July 1904).

John W. Goff wanted to go on the ship with full authority over captain and crew, a proposal which was firmly rejected, because in this he would be assuming a capacity for which he was obviously not fitted. A number of men were sounded about their willingness to take part, without definitely selecting any of them, and it worked out in the end that there were far more volunteers than there were places available for them. One of the committee's greatest difficulties was to choose the most suitable men and appease the others. Some were very discomfited at not being let take part and their dissatisfaction gave no end of trouble.

The official report of the Australian Prisoners Rescue Committee, dated at Philadelphia, 9 August 1876, gives the following account of the situation facing the committee at the end of the first six months of preparation:

The subscriptions came in slowly and the project met with much opposition in many branches, but finally, when it was ascertained that from six to seven thousand dollars had been raised, a meeting of the committee was called and the matter laid before it. Seeing that there was not money enough to purchase and fit out a ship, it was thought that a bargain might be made with a whaler to call at a port agreed on in Western Australia and take the men on board when agents sent by steamer beforehand should have effected a rescue. The difficulties in the way were clearly seen, and the danger of failing to connect with a ship which could be more profitably employed in whaling than in waiting for the chance of a successful rescue was a source of anxiety, but for want of funds no other plan seemed then feasible.

It was at this stage that they decided on John Boyle O'Reilly's suggestion to seek advice from Captain Henry C. Hathaway of New Bedford. He had whaled over the seven seas and knew the Indian Ocean and the west Australian coast like the palm of his hand. Besides, he was the man chiefly instrumental in rescuing O'Reilly from his captivity in Western Australia. So the Rescue Committee appointed

John Devoy and Jim Reynolds to go and see Hathaway and talk the matter over with him, find out from him the probable cost of sending a ship to Australia and any other views he might have on the project.

CHAPTER TEN

HATHAWAY OF NEW BEDFORD

DEVOY left New York on Friday, 29 January 1875, for New Bedford, Massachusetts, breaking his journey in New Haven to talk matters over with Jim Reynolds and bring him along if he was free. Reynolds was unable to go with him so Devoy set out alone, on Saturday night, for Boston. He wanted first to see John Boyle O'Reilly, between whom and Hathaway there was the closest friendship and mutual confidence, and get a letter of introduction from O'Reilly to Hathaway. On reaching Boston, Devoy called to see the officers of the Celtic club, as the local Clan na Gael body was known, and during conversation with them found they were strongly prejudiced against O'Reilly. A few years before that O'Reilly, Robert Dwyer Joyce, Patrick Collins and John E. Fitzgerald had resigned from the organisation, at the request of the Archbishop of Boston, it was said, and there was strong feeling against them in Clan na Gael circles for doing so. They were thought to have abandoned the Irish cause.

To anyone who looks back on the careers of these men the charge is baseless. In the case of O'Reilly it is ludicrous. Few men have ever attained to the affection and esteem in which he was, and is, held throughout America. The long entry by which he is honoured in the *Dictionary of American Biography*, the appraisal of his notable democratic and liberal stature in Arthur Mann's *Yankee Reformers in the Urban Age*, his fine and sensitive portrait in the most recent biography (1958) by William Schofield, the tribute from hundreds of eminent men in his own day, the wave of grief at his tragic and early death, all bear witness that he was one of the great men in whom Irish patriotism and American idealism united to form an admirable blend. He was now editor of the diocesan paper, *The Pilot*, which he conducted with a balance and integrity that did justice to the highest standards of journalism.

Devoy sensed at once that he was not popular with Clan na Gael in Boston. Very wisely he said nothing to the Clan officers about his mission. More than twenty years after, one of the members of the Celtic club reproached Devoy for keeping them in ignorance of it while he told all to O'Reilly. Devoy's practical mind saw that this was the proper thing to do. We find the following entry in his diary for Monday, February 1, 1875:

> Called on O'Reilly and Cashman at *Pilot* office. Told O'Reilly my business. He offered to come with me and introduce me to Hathaway if I could wait till Tuesday, Monday being his busy day. Gladly consented, knowing his influence with Hathaway. Spent evening at his house, talking over his escape, etc., Cashman with us.

But when Devoy called on O'Reilly at the *Pilot* office next day he found him in bad humour, because an ex-prisoner to whom he had lent a large sum of money had gone bankrupt. His present worries and business did not permit him to accompany Devoy, but he wrote a letter introducing him to Hathaway in the most earnest terms. With this in his pocket, Devoy started for New Bedford that evening. The entry in his diary for next day (February) reads:

> Stopped at Parker House. Had some delay in finding Hathaway. When I gave him O'Reilly's note saw a good effect produced at once. It was in the police station. He is captain of night police. Told me quietly to follow him. Went into courthouse and locked door. Sat down and talked whole thing over. Entered warmly into project. Found he knew all about our men. Recommended strongly the buying of a vessel and gave solid reasons why any other course would not be safe. Showed how it could be made to pay expenses. Splendid physique; handsome, honest face; quite English-looking. Wears only side-whiskers; very reserved in manner; speaks low and slowly, but every word fits. Never without a cigar in his mouth. Eighteen years to sea, whaling all the time.

Devoy's terse description of Hathaway shows that here he

had located a very real asset to their enterprise, a man of clear and practical mind who could visualise success if everything was properly handled. Devoy's obvious confidence in him is further acknowledged in the letter he wrote that same day to Jim Reynolds:

> I have seen the man I expected and found him to be up to my highest expectations.—(*Devoy's Post Bag,* I, 88).

Devoy remained some time in New Bedford, under an assumed name, and called on Hathaway every morning and evening to discuss the project, and wrote the substance of what Hathaway recommended to the other members of the committee. What Hathaway recommended gave the whole project a decisive and firm direction which was hitherto lacking, and placed in clear perspective the problems that had to be faced. In his eighteen years of experience as a whaler, Hathaway had acquired a thorough knowledge of Western Australia and the Indian Ocean. He recommended that a ship should be bought, fitted out as a whaler, a trustworthy captain put on board and sent out to Western Australia. He explained how a ship like that could pay its own way and even make a profit if the whaling was very good. He put the cost at 12,000 dollars for a small ship undertaking one year's voyage. He gave reasons why it would be far better for the Clan na Gael to be themselves the owners of the ship going on such an enterprise. To rely on others was risky and uncertain. No ship would be sailing for those parts for several months, and in no instance, out of the many ships he knew of, could he vouch for the good faith and honesty of the captain. He pointed out, too, that a whaler was likely to change course according to his success in whaling. Since the value of two good whales would be far more than the Rescue Committee could then offer as a reward for doing the work, it was taking too great a risk to entrust the work to a captain who might be tempted to abandon it in favour of good whale fishing.

The new light in which the captain placed the whole question greatly impressed Devoy. He wrote the substance of

Hathaway's advice to the other members of the committee and recommended a change in the original half-shaped plan. The situation which faced them now was that they had nothing like enough money on hand to purchase and equip a whaler, not to mention sending agents ahead by steamer as well. The appeals for voluntary subscriptions had so far brought in only about $7,000, which was little more than half the amount suggested as necessary by Captain Hathaway, and since these appeals had been as urgent and strongly worded as possible it was very unlikely that any fresh appeal would bring in the required balance. Besides, Captain Hathaway's estimate was not a definite one. It did not relate to a particular ship, but was made on the general basis of fitting out a ship costing $4,000 for a twelve months' cruise. The actual cost might well be more. Devoy considered that in these circumstances they should ask such clubs as had large funds to lend a portion of them for the rescue, and he had no doubt that these loans could be repaid by the profits from the whaling. It will be remembered that there was a revolutionary fund in existence totalling at that time about $42,000, distributed throughout the different branches of Clan na Gael, and closely held against the day when the call of revolution in Ireland made a demand on it. John Devoy now decided to ask the Rescue Committee to appeal to the organisation for the necessary amount from this revolutionary fund, leaving it optional with the branches to give the money or not, and if they voted any, leaving the amount to their own discretion. Any attempt to levy a pro rata amount on the clubs would not work, and would not be acceptable to some of them, because it was known that some clubs were hostile to the project of rescue in any shape, and many others were lukewarm or inactive through want of confidence. He recommended that the appeal should be most directly made to such clubs as had large funds.

Devoy realised that this new appeal would involve fresh risks that some hint of the project might leak out to the British authorities through indiscretion or plain spying, but the risks had to be run or the task abandoned. A great deal of allowance was made for the fact that, after the Fenian fiascos, the British authorities entertained a profound contempt for the ability of the Clan to bring an enterprise to success. Devoy, working away ruthlessly, wrote to every member of the committee and placed the full facts, and his recommendations, before him. After a short time, replies in agreement with his views came from all. Circulars were at once sent out appealing for the necessary funds. There followed a period of anxiety and uncertainty for the committee, the burthen of which fell mainly on Devoy, as to whether enough money to start the expedition would come in or not. Many were the refusals, disappointments and frustrations experienced.

The Clan branches voted the funds in due course, although in some cases there was considerable trouble and delay. Some trustees proved obstinate and refused to draw funds which branches had voted. There were many other delays and difficulties. Two very earnest Fenians, who were trustees of Devoy's own branch of the Clan, refused point blank to draw the $2,500 voted by an overwhelming majority. They had to be removed from office and replaced by two others before the money could be got. In Louisville, Kentucky, where the Clan na Gael was very strong, Michael Boland, who was trustee there, held up a large sum in the same way. Eventually, however, all the money voted was made available to the Australian Rescue Committee.

CHAPTER ELEVEN

BUYING A SHIP

THE Rescue Committee asked Captain Hathaway to be on the look out for a suitable ship that might be for sale and to recommend a whaling agent who could be entrusted with the assignment of getting the vessel ready for sea. Hathaway wrote in February to say that a suitable ship was on the market, that she would probably cost $6,000 and could be fitted out for as much more. He gave her inventory, which was good. Here was a chance of securing a good ship if only the cash for it was on hand. Unfortunately it was not. Devoy and his colleagues were aware that the sooner they bought a ship the better, because towards the approach of May prices would be going up with the increasing demand in spring for ships. So they tried to buy this one.

Captain Hathaway said he might be able to delay the sale for a few days to give them time, and as the matter was urgent, Devoy telegraphed him at once to try and delay sale till 1 March. He wrote to Hathaway at the same time to say that parties authorised by the committee would go to New Bedford on 1 March, and if the ship suited and the price was reasonable she would be bought and half the amount paid in cash, the balance to be paid in as short a time afterwards as would be mutually agreed.

The six members of the committee who resided near enough to attend meetings were telegraphed at once, and written to as well, so that as many of them as possible might be present to take part in the purchase and that those who could not go might authorise the others to act on their behalf. None was found able to go except Devoy and Goff, but the others all agreed to leave the matter in the hands of whoever went and gave them full authority to act on their behalf. Devoy and Goff decided, with the consent of the other four, to take two well-trusted members of the Clan na Gael, outside the committee, along with them to be witnesses in the transactions. The purpose of this was to protect Devoy and Goff from any possible charges of irregular dealing. There had been exposures in the organisation the year before, involving the misuse of revolutionary funds, and the secretary of the Clan, W. J. Nicholson, had been dismissed from the organisation for a transaction in which he was really more unfortunate than blameworthy. The handling of money was therefore a sensitive subject, and the members of the committee felt bound to place their acts in the clearest light.

The two non-committee members selected to go with Devoy and Goff were Miles O'Brien and James Muldoon. The party travelled to New Bedford on 1 March, arriving only to meet with disappointment. The ship had been sold the day before. Devoy, writing to Jim Reynolds from New Bedford on 2 March 1875, says:

My Dear R,

We got here yesterday morning—too late to secure the ship we expected to get, and we must wait a few days longer. It went for $6,300. Others, suitable enough, but not having so good an inventory, are to be got, but we must have the money on hand.

We have lodged up to to-day, $2,000 in the hands of Hathaway, and an agent who is trustworthy, and our friends must hand up the remainder so as to enable us to buy *this week,* as it will take six weeks to get her ready for sea.

Goff and two New York men, Miles O'Brien of D.13, and James Muldoon, S.G., of D.150, who is a marine engineer doing business in Washington St., were the only men that came, and all but myself have gone home. I will stay here till a ship is bought.

D. No. 1 [Devoy's own club] voted $1,500 dollars last night and $1,000 more if required. How is that for spirit?

I will keep you posted as I go along. Remember me to all.

Yours, J.D.

—(*Devoy's Post Bag,* I, p. 95).

In New Bedford, Captain Hathaway introduced them to John T. Richardson, a whaling agent, whom he had previously recommended as the best man to act in the enterprise in that capacity. Richardson was a native of Virginia but had lived since boyhood in New Bedford. The Clan na Gael men took him into the secret, told him all about their object in buying a ship and appointed him to act as agent on their behalf. He sympathised fully and with sturdy Yankee spirit went into the enterprise, fully aware of the risks it involved. He was asked to look out for a suitable ship so that the work could be begun as soon as possible. An initial sum of $1,500 was deposited with Richardson as a first instalment against the cost of a vessel. O'Brien, Muldoon and Goff spoke in the highest terms of Richardson, fully approved the arrangements made with him and returned to New York the same evening.

Devoy remained on in New Bedford in order to pay Richardson the money according as it was forwarded, and Richardson gave Devoy receipts specifying that the money was deposited for the purpose of "purchasing a whaling bark." The members of the committee were all written to and consulted about everything that was done. Nearly always it was Devoy who did the writing, with the result that his eyesight, none too good already because of damage wrought on it by prison conditions, suffered badly from the strain. Methodical, persevering and dauntless, to him belongs the main credit for bringing the enterprise step by step forward with persistent tenacity. He writes to Reynolds:

I have not a solitary minute to myself. This thing must be made a success at all hazards.—(*Devoy's Post Bag*, I, p. 96).

He strongly urged the Rescue Committee to hurry up the various sums collected and not yet turned in, but in spite of their best efforts there was a lot of frustrating delay caused by the slackness of some officers in sending on the money.

After a good deal of bargaining and examination of various ships, the *Catalpa*, which was then lying at east Boston, was bought for $5,250. She was 202 tons net, ninety feet long, twenty-five wide and just over twelve deep. Formerly a whaling vessel sailing out of New Bedford, she had been converted into a merchant ship and was only back with a cargo of logwood from the West Indies. The bill of sale was made out in John T. Richardson's name, so that no suspicion might be aroused about the real object of her purchase. Writing from New Bedford to Reynolds on 11 March 1875, Devoy announces the purchase and describes their difficulties about money:

We have bought a vessel and she must be paid for by Saturday. The amount is $5,250, and there are some fees, pilotage to this port, ballast, etc., to be paid besides, and some of the outfit and stores already bought. All we have on hand is $4,900. The $1,500 of D.1, partly through sulk on the part of two of the trustees, partly, Goff says, through the S.G.'s neglect, has not come in yet, and no districts but A and F have yet sent anything. If we had the necessary funds now she could be ready for sea in three weeks. I could get $7,000 for her if I agreed to sell her, as she was not advertised for sale and is coveted by a man for the West India trade . . . Keep this matter quiet, as we must move with great caution now.

Yours, J.D.

—(*Devoy's Post Bag*, I, p. 97).

The bill of sale of the *Catalpa* is dated 27 April 1875, and bears the signature of James C. Hitch, Registrar of the Sales and Transfers at the Custom House in New Bedford. It records the purchase of the vessel by John T. Richardson from F. W. Homan, Gloucester, Mass., states her dimensions and the fact that she was built at Medford in 1844, with other details of interest. The transfer to James Reynolds is stated in the quaint language of legal documents:

> To have and to hold the said seven-eighths bark Catalpa and appurtenances thereunto belonging to him, the said James Reynolds, his executors, administrators and assigns, to the sole and only proper use, benefit and behoof of him the said James Reynolds, etc.

Jim Reynolds, "Catalpa Jim," thus became managing owner of the ship, holding seven-eighths possession of her. It was vital to secure immediate possession of this ship and commence fitting her out, and the requisite cash had not been on hand. In fact, Richardson had to advance $4,000 of his own money for the purchase, and Jim Reynolds, on his own responsibility, went security that he would be refunded. The note by which he secured Richardson survived the vicissitudes of time and reads as follows:

> New Bedford,
>
> $4,000 April 27, 1875.
>
> Thirty days after date I promise to pay to the order of John T. Richardson, at the Mechanics National Bank, Four Thousand Dollars, Value Received.
>
> James Reynolds.

On the back of the note are recorded payments beginning 29 April and ending 24 May 1875, amounting to $4,364.41, so that the incoming Clan na Gael funds redeemed it within the thirty days.

Along with Richardson and Devoy when they went to east Boston to inspect the *Catalpa* was a man who was to play a vital part in the rescue. He was George S. Anthony, Richardson's son-in-law. A native of New Bedford, he had gone to sea at fifteen and learned all there was to know about whaling. Experienced, steady and reliable, he had spent ten years on one ship for agent Jonathan Bourne, a man who held him in great regard. Now at 29 years of age and married happily to John T. Richardson's daughter, he had decided to settle down on shore and was employed in an engineering works in New Bedford at the time Devoy was visiting the city on his ship-buying mission. But a restless yearning for the sea kept prompting him, and his father-in-law hinted to him that an exciting job was coming up in which he might be interested. He asked George Anthony to come on a certain evening to his store on 18 South Water Street to meet the parties who would tell him all about it.

At the meeting, Richardson introduced his son-in-law to Devoy, Goff and Reynolds. Also present was Captain Hathaway. Devoy addressed himself to George Anthony and began to talk. He outlined the history of the Fenian movement and explained that it was an effort, one of many over the centuries, to achieve the freedom of a nation. He told how a small group of men, participants in the effort, now languished in Fremantle jail, and that it was proposed to liberate them by sending out a whaling vessel which would pick them up, at a certain time, at an agreed point off the Australian coast. The shore end of the rescue would be managed by others. Would he, Anthony, command the rescue vessel and go on this dangerous rescue expedition?

This briefly was the proposition put up to the astonished young seaman. After considering it for a short time he decided to accept it. It would be superfluous to say that George S. Anthony was a brave man to set out on this fantastic and perilous adventure. He was not bound to Ireland by any ties of blood or kin. He was happily married with a bonny baby daughter. Without any doubt he could get other berths which would be secure and satisfactory. Behind his decision lay the proud traditions of New Bedford history and seamanship, his great human sympathy for soldiers of freedom in captive toils, his Yankee respect for liberty, and his personal attribute of superb courage. His mind once made up, he went into the adventure with a serene and steady resolve to carry it through to success. It was a challenge.

A New Bedford sailor to balk at danger! Never! And it was his first command. Henceforth he was Captain George S. Anthony, master of the whaling bark *Catalpa.*

CHAPTER TWELVE

FITTING OUT THE *CATALPA*

DEVOY decided to take no risks as to the quality and seaworthiness of the craft. As soon as Richardson and Captain Anthony had returned to New Bedford, Lieutenant Tobin, a United States naval engineer who was on duty at the Boston naval yard, and who had been introduced to Devoy by John Boyle O'Reilly, was taken on board the *Catalpa* to give the ship a thorough examination.

Devoy's meeting with Tobin took place in a historic setting, and is described as follows by the Fenian leader:

> He and I dined at O'Reilly's house in Charlestown under the shadow of Bunker Hill on the Sunday after the purchase of the *Catalpa.* O'Reilly had introduced me under my proper name, told him I had been in prison for Fenianism with him, that I represented a firm that was going to embark on the fruit trade and, as I knew nothing about shipping, he would be greatly obliged if he would come over and take a look at the vessel. Lieutenant Tobin entered into the examination with great zest, never for a moment suspecting our object.

With a jack-knife he cut out pieces of her timber for testing, and made every other necessary check. His verdict was that, although a little old, she was a sound craft, fit to sail anywhere. The only drawback, in his opinion, was that she was a slow sailer. On being asked what did he think her worth, he could not say for certain as the markets varied such a lot. At a guess he would put her value at $7,000 at least, but thought she might well have cost $8,000 or even $10,000. When told the actual price he said she was a genuine bargain. Many years later Lieutenant Tobin called to see John Devoy in New York and told him that if he had known the purpose for which the vessel was intended he could not have carried out the examination, but that he was very glad he did not know and that the expedition turned out a success. A splendid fellow, thought Devoy, and hoped he would yet be an admiral.

The *Catalpa* was taken to New Bedford wharf as soon as the ice began to thaw, and the work of fitting her out as a whaler was begun without delay. Many important changes had to be made before she could set out on a whaling voyage. A blubber deck had to be constructed, a furnace and trying apparatus had to be installed, and a great number of minor changes were needed. These sent costs up. She had to be coppered, whaling boats had to be built, and some extra boats were required for the use of the men who would be rescued. For economy, these were bought secondhand, tested for soundness and repaired. Sails, anchor, chronometer and a great deal else had to be ordered, and the cost of every item was duly recorded. The chronometer, incidentally, proved to be defective and gave Captain Anthony a great deal of trouble during the voyage. Stores, oil and water casks, harpoons, bomb-lances, and medicine chest were duly put on board. The fitting-out of the vessel was superintended from start to finish by Captain Hathaway, whose help and advice, freely and generously given, were an immense advantage. Hathaway's eighteen years' whaling experience was a great asset to agent Richardson, and many things which were usually put on board a whaler were left out on his advice that they were not really needed. He saved the Clan na Gael a great deal of expense by this, and the *Catalpa* was, under his direction, fitted out efficiently but cheaply. There were critics who were only too ready to say, as they did, that the work had been done at an extravagant and reckless cost, but the vouchers were there to refute them.

The fitting out of the ship took a lot of time and the expense was a good deal higher than the committee had anticipated, having regard to Hathaway's original estimate of $12,000. Devoy had to make several trips from New York to New Bedford, and, as costs went up, he had in turn to visit several Clan na Gael centres to urge the voting of more money to make up the deficiency. It was a vexatious and thankless task. Invariably when men heard the cost would be much more than the first estimate, they carped, bristled and grumbled. There were delays and suspicions, making the task of the committee more difficult and making heavy demands on their time, especially Devoy's and Reynolds's. Devoy was never without his critics. He was not exactly a diplomat, and very often he rubbed people the wrong way, but he got things done. A contemporary report says of him:

> The master spirit of the affair was John Devoy, who may be said to have done all the working in America, from the organising of the Irish nationalists for the business to seeing it fairly under its way for its destination.—(*United Irishman*, Liverpool, 26 August 1876).

Always present was the fear that a hint might leak out to the British authorities and ruin all. A subsequent report of the Australian Prisoners Rescue Committee strongly recommended that, in any future enterprise of this kind, there should be sufficient confidence in those in office at the time to give them ample funds, without having to take the risk of giving vital information to a very large number of people, amongst whom might be spies or careless talkers.

Even the New Bedford experts had not allowed for enough in their estimate, and this letter of Hathaway's to Devoy indicates the need for more funds, or "fodder" as he calls it in his very cautious way of putting things.

New Bedford,
March 15, 1875.

To John Devoy Esq.,

Dear Sir: You perhaps noticed my short stay in Boston in the presence of J.B.O'R. I could have stayed a short time longer, but for fear we might be overheard as he talked pretty loud.

I hope you had a good look at the *Horse* in Charleston and was satisfied with it. I think it's a tip-top bargain. I liked the looks of him first-rate and think he will bring more than we paid for him any day. We have already been offered $1,000 more than we paid for him, but think he will more than pay for himself this coming season on the track. We are going for him this week. The weather is now very favorable, and think we can get him here by Thurs. or Fri. I think he will cost us nearly $7,000, but we will try to do our best and make everything count. We have commenced this morning in earnest and will pay for the Horse to-day. I hope you will be punctual in sending us the fodder, as grain is on the rise here.

Please give my compliments to those other men, and hasten things as soon as possible.

Mr. R. sends his compliments. How did you like the looks of the man that we chose to take charge of the Horse? He is the right man for it.

Yours in haste,

H.C.H.
Capt.

It was an indication of Hathaway's caution that he spoke of the *Catalpa* as a "horse." This was wise, because too many instances had occurred to show that the United States mails were not sacrosanct. His reference to O'Reilly talking loud was another sign of his caution, though the talk took place in O'Reilly's Boston *Pilot* office, with nobody present except the trusted James Jeffrey Roche, assistant editor and Denis B. Cashman, himself an ex-prisoner of Fremantle. The "man to take charge of the Horse" was, of course, Captain Anthony, and never was confidence more fully borne out.

Reynolds of New Haven, who was the member of the committee living nearest to New Bedford, was kept constantly informed of the progress of the outfitting, and of the soaring costs. Richardson, writing to him from New Bedford on 16 April, states:

Dear Friend and Partner,

I have this moment received your check for $4,344.30, for which I send you this receipt.

J. T. Richardson.

The ship is now coppered and off the ways all ready for stowing and painting. It will take but a few days to finish up everything. The ship will sail for a great deal more than what we first anticipated, but we have a ship that we can depend on and one that will bring a good price any day when we are ready to sell. I hope that won't be for some time for she is worth as much to us as to anybody else. I am in hopes at the end of the voyage to show you that this is the business to invest money in, and furthermore I am confident that your wish will be granted in regards to those men in Western Australia.

I think the vessel will sail for over $17,000 and I will be ready to meet my share of the expenses at any day when the bills are all in. I hope you will be punctual in forwarding more money as soon as possible, and when I send for you to come to N.B. you will be prepared to settle all bills, as we have agreed with all who I have bought goods off to pay cash. I think now the 26th of this month will be the day for her sailing. Please answer immediately and let me know what your expectations are in regards to the full amount.

I don't want to keep the ship waiting a moment after she is ready for sea as her expenses will be heavy for each day she is detained, as some of her crew live in other places far from here, and if the ship is not ready to sail when they come it will create dissatisfaction with them. Besides it will cost a great deal to keep them waiting.

Yours truly,
J. T. Richardson.

—(*Devoy's Post Bag*, I, p. 103).

Finally the vessel was ready. Hathaway wrote to Reynolds on 22 April 1875:

To James Reynolds Esq.,
New Haven, Conn.

Dear Sir, Mr. Richardson is very busy fitting the ship and wishes me to answer your letter. He says the vessel will go to sea next Tuesday morning, April 27th, without fail, as it will not do to detain her after she is ready, for several reasons, he wishes me to state that the amount that will be required for ship and outfits will be about $18,000.

This is a great deal more than we expected to sail for in the first place; but we have been as prudent as possible and bought everything at the lowest market price, and bought nothing but what is actually required for the voyage. I hope you and Mr. Devoy will be here in time to see her go, for I want you to see her as she is fitted for sea. You have got a good ship. Mr. Richardson is about buying another ship to be fitted shortly for the Atlantic Ocean.

I placed myself in a queer position when I placed this job in the hands of Mr. Richardson, and although I am busy and anxious every day, there is quite a load taken from my shoulders by your visit to New Bedford, though I have the same interest now as ever.

Perhaps you had better telegraph to Mr. Devoy at once and be here by Sunday, or Monday sure, as there will be no delay in her sailing.

Please let me know by telegraph when you will be here.

Yours truly,
Henry C. Hathaway.

But even Hathaway's eve of sailing estimate was below the

mark. Item by item, the cost of the *Catalpa* and its outfitting was as follows, according to the receipted bills covering the entire transaction:

Ship	$5,250
Carpenter Work	1,500
Coppering	1,600
Beef & Pork	1,130
Flour	700
Stewards Outfit	300
Small stores	800
Casks	1,550
Irons	700
Boats	420
Sails	50
Sail making	145
Cordage	500
Paint, etc.	265
Labor, wharfage, etc.	700
	$15,610
Advances and outfits	3,400
Total	$19,010

This was well in excess of Hathaway's original estimate of $12,000.

CHAPTER THIRTEEN

THE VOYAGE BEGINS

THE announcement by Richardson that the vessel was ready for sea faced the Rescue Committee with a new question that had to be solved without delay. It was agreed with Anthony, Hathaway and Richardson that one or two Clan na Gael men were to be included in the crew of the *Catalpa*. There were plenty willing to go, but the selection had to be confined to two at most. Captain Anthony was for having only one. The ship's crew selected by Anthony was mainly composed of Malays, Sandwich Island Kanakas, Portuguese Negroes from the Azores and Cape Verde Islands. They were a normal crew for a whaling voyage. If they had a suspicion that something other than whaling was on foot the whole plan would collapse at once. If any one was taken on board who did not fit into a legitimate shipboard job he would naturally arouse suspicion.

The committee had gradually narrowed down the number of men who were eager to go. Originally twelve or fifteen, the choice was now reduced to four. These were Denis Duggan, Thomas Brennan, John O'Connor and Harry Mulleda.

Hathaway, Richardson and Captain Anthony had all along argued that one Clan na Gael man would be enough, but that if two were found to be necessary they would have to fill the positions of steward and carpenter. The steward would have to know all about cooking and catering for the crew. Anyone without that knowledge trying to fill the position would have a very unpleasant time. John O'Connor offered to take on the job; he had the necessary skill, but he made it a condition that Harry Mulleda came with him as carpenter. Mulleda, who was engaged to be married and was between two minds whether to go or not, finally decided not to, so John O'Connor also withdrew. There remained Duggan and Brennan. Duggan was a coachbuilder who had turned his skill to carpentry. A native of Dublin, he had been with Devoy at School Street Model Schools. His valour was not in doubt. He was one of Stephens's bodyguard on the night of the latter's liberation from Richmond bridewell, Dublin, in November 1865, and in the 1867 rising he had fought at Stepaside and Glencullen in the Dublin mountains. Tom Brennan was also a Dublin man and likewise a classmate of Devoy's at an earlier period in Marlborough Street Schools. He, too, had fought on the Dublin hills and his courage was well proved.

Devoy recommended Duggan because he was a carpenter and therefore had the most useful training for the job. In this Devoy had the written votes of all the members of the committee in favour of his selection except one. That one was John W. Goff who presently became a severe critic of all the arrangements which had been carried out by Devoy.

Devoy still hoped, however, that Brennan could be taken on board in some capacity.

Reynolds sent on to Devoy the final letter from Hathaway announcing that the ship was ready to sail. Devoy wrote to Goff at once, telling him of the situation, and on the Monday evening before the ship sailed Goff replied:

Dear John,

Just received your note. Will get the committee together as soon as possible. Would like to go down myself. From what you tell me I presume Duggan to be a good man and fitted. I would prefer that not one man be taken from New York if you can get along without.

Between John O'Connor and Brennan, my choice is Brennan . . . I will see Brennan at once.

Fraternally,

[Signed in cipher].

It was obvious that Goff was going to propose Brennan. Devoy started at once for New Bedford. Reynolds was there before him and had already solved the question of who should go on board. Reynolds was owner-manager of the *Catalpa* and therefore in a position of authority to make the decision which was at once put up to him. At the urgent request of Richardson, Anthony and Hathaway, he had solved the difficulty on the spot by agreeing with them that only one Clan na Gael man should go on board and that Duggan was the man. Accordingly, Duggan was already installed as ship's carpenter when Devoy arrived on the scene. Reynolds knew that in solving the situation in this way he had the confidence of nearly all his colleagues. Devoy endorsed his action. The vessel was now cleared and her papers, including a full list of her officers and crew, had been recorded in New Bedford customs house.

The day he arrived in New Bedford, Devoy got a telegram from Goff stating that Tom Brennan must be taken aboard and that he would bring him down to the dock the following morning. Goff and his protege arrived, to be told that Duggan had been installed as carpenter and the ship's papers cleared.

They were both highly indignant at this. It was the beginning of a pique on the part of Goff, which was to lead to a great deal of trouble. Reynolds and Devoy stood firm in their decision. They could do this. They both had the written authorisation of the rest of their committee colleagues to act for them, and the two of them had been appointed a sub-committee to manage the business subject to the control of all the other members. There was no quarrel and no angry words were spoken, but the situation was strained as they all stood there on the dock that morning of 29 April and talked the matter over. A quarrel now would have a bad effect, and an alteration of the ship's papers, or any attempt to place on board an extra man who did not fit in, would have disastrous results.

Captain Hathaway, resourceful as usual, suggested a way out of the difficulty. All whalers, he said, were liable to have a man die during the voyage, or desert on reaching the Azores, and in this way a vacancy might arise. If Brennan could be sent to Fayal or St. Michael's in the Azores, to contact the *Catalpa* on its arrival there, then Captain Anthony could take him on board or not, according to his judgment or discretion, and it would solve the problem. They talked it over and agreed to this. It was later discussed and ratified by the whole Rescue Committee, and a letter of instructions for Brennan was drafted by Devoy. These instructions explicitly directed him, in the name of the governing body of Clan na Gael, to abide by Captain Anthony's decision in Fayal. After their agreement on this basis, made on New Bedford dock, they all went on board the *Catalpa* and sailed out into Buzzard's bay. After a meal on board, Devoy, Goff, Brennan and the others said farewell to Captain Anthony and returned to New Bedford dock in a whaleboat. Of the numerous family friends of the captain who came down to the dock or went out to the ship to wish him bon voyage, not one was aware of the real purpose of the cruise.

John Devoy has left many letters and other writings, and his style is direct, clear and functional. The following letter contains one of the very rare passages in which he permitted himself to be lyrical. It was written from New Bedford to Jim Reynolds on the evening of Thursday, 29 April 1875, the day the *Catalpa* began her voyage.

My Dear R.

Goff, Brennan and I have just returned from seeing the ship forty miles out to sea, eating our dinner of hard tack, salt beef and cheese aboard. She looked splendid, with every sail set, a clear sky overhead and a calm sea beneath, and the scene at parting was one we shall not soon forget. About thirty men, all excepting our three being friends of agent, captain or officers, went out in a yacht, got on board and remained there till she was well out, giving three hearty cheers, with the usual "tiger," for the barque and her crew. Not a man but ourselves had the least suspicion of her mission, and she is well on her way now . . .

J.D.

—(*Devoy's Post Bag*, I, page 105).

So Captain Anthony set out on his extraordinary quest. Devoy and his colleagues on New Bedford dock watched the vessel go down behind the horizon. Goff claimed he could still see it when it had sailed beyond the vision of everyone else. He considered Devoy's eyesight defective.

Devoy and his companions were tired men that evening, but they had the satisfaction of having completed the first stage of their daring design. They rested the night in New Bedford. Next day they got down to dealing with the less exciting but important business of checking the bills and expenditure of the project. This was turning out to be much larger than they had expected.

CHAPTER FOURTEEN

BRESLIN AND DESMOND SAIL TO AUSTRALIA

SOON after the *Catalpa* sailed a meeting of the Rescue Committee was held to select the man who was to go direct to Fremantle to carry out the first stage of the rescue, that is to say, from the prison itself. At first Devoy intended to go personally, and states he was assured of all the votes of the committee except one, the one presumably being Goff, and he was not even sure of that one being against him. He finally decided against going, giving as the reason that:

> Conditions arose, owing to impatience and dissatisfaction on the part of men who had helped to raise the money, which made it absolutely necessary that I should remain in New York. In fact, my disappearance would have at once indicated that I had gone to Australia and the consequent loose talk would almost certainly have ruined [the] chances of success. I gave up the idea very reluctantly, mainly at the request of Mahon and Reynolds.—(*Gaelic American*, 27 August 1904).

Devoy knew a man who would be fit in every way for the assignment. A short time before this John J. Breslin had left Boston to come and live in New York. He was an unobtrusive, modest man who shunned the limelight. Very few in New York knew he had come, and very few, if any, would take notice if he left again. He had obvious qualifications for the difficult job in Fremantle. It was he who had planned in every detail the liberation of the Fenian chief, James Stephens, from Richmond prison in Dublin, and he had taken the main part in it himself. His long experience of the British prison service would be useful. Breslin had a fine appearance, good manners, a natural courtesy, keen intelligence and a prompt and decisive mind. Devoy thought he was the ideal man for the work. There was a difficulty to be got over, however. Hardly any of the members of the Rescue Committee knew him, except Devoy, who knew him very well, and Goff, whose acquaintance with him was slight. Not only was he not a member of Clan na Gael but he belonged to a rival organisation, the U.I.B., of which only two branches existed, one in Boston and one in New York. At a conference held to bring about a union, which was not effected, between the two organisations, he had met Goff along with Devoy. His record pointed to him as the very man for the task and when sounded about it he expressed his willingness. In the course of the negotiations with him someone committed a blunder, however. To suggest to a quiet, proud man like him that he would be selected only on condition that he joined

Clan na Gael was inviting certain rejection of the offer. Yet when Devoy proposed him for the chief command of the expedition that very condition was tactlessly made. After some diplomatic approaches Breslin was at last sworn quietly into the organisation in Hoboken, and all obstacles were removed. The committee unanimously approved his selection.

Nearly half the money collected for the rescue project had been raised by the California Clan na Gael. Talbot of San Francisco had, without question or demur, performed wonders by his enthusiasm. California Clan na Gael now made a very earnest request. It was that one of the California organisation should be permitted to take part in the rescue, selection of the man to be made by John C. Talbot. The committee agreed to this, and Talbot chose Tom Desmond, who accompanied Breslin to Australia and proved himself a plucky, intrepid and valuable assistant.

The method of effecting the rescue was left to the full discretion of Breslin, who was to use his own judgment on the spot in the face of whatever situation confronted him. But after the rescue was effected there were clear and explicit instructions as to the disposal of the vessel and rescued men. The same instructions had been given to Captain Anthony. They were that the rescued men were to be landed at Fernandina, Florida. This done, the *Catalpa* was to put to sea again to cruise in the Atlantic for whales, so as to clear if possible the expenses of the expedition and pay back the money given out of the revolutionary funds to the committee by a large number of clubs.

There was a good reason for choosing Fernandina as the port where the rescued men were to be landed. United States Senator S. B. Conover, of Florida, was a member of the Clan na Gael, although both he and his parents were born in America. His grandfather, an Ulster Presbyterian, had taken part in the insurrection of 1798 and had to flee to America for safety. The Senator's strong sentiments in favour of Ireland were derived from the family tradition. During the Civil War, Conover had been a surgeon in the Union army where, in the course of his service, he met Dr. William

Carroll, who later brought him into the Clan na Gael. The collector of customs at Fernandina was a friend of Conover's and was to make all the arrangements for receiving the rescued men, while the *Catalpa* put to sea again to continue whaling.

Breslin left New York early on 19 July 1875 and travelled by the Lake Shore and Michigan southern route to San Francisco. His instructions were to organise the rescue of the six prisoners James Wilson, Martin J. Hogan, Michael Harrington, Robert Cranston, Thomas Hassett and Thomas Darragh, or as many of them as he could, to use his own judgment as to the means and manner of the rescue, to expect the *Catalpa* in January 1876 and to complete the rescue in co-operation with its captain. He arrived in San Francisco on 26 July 1875. Talbot was away in Sacramento, and Breslin, after a few days' delay, set out to see him, travelling by steamer up the Sacramento river and arriving on the morning of the 30th. He handed Talbot a letter of introduction from John Devoy. Talbot telegraphed to John Kenealy in Los Angeles that Breslin had arrived and Kenealy sent Thomas Desmond to Sacramento to meet him. Before leaving New York, Breslin had been told by Devoy that they had granted the request of the California Clan na Gael to be allowed to send a man along with him to assist in the rescue. Breslin said that unless he approved of the man he would not have him, and Devoy thought that was fair enough. Breslin likewise told Talbot at their first meeting that unless the man was one he could trust and work with he would reject him. Talbot agreed that that was reasonable, but added that they had chosen the very best man they had, "and I think you will like him."

Desmond arrived in Sacramento a few days afterwards and at once made a good impression on Breslin who, in his report to the Clan, after the rescue had been effected, paid him the following generous tribute:

> I now believe that if Desmond alone had been sent, the rescue would have been as successfully accomplished, and at far less cost to the organisation; for while my expenses, from the position I had

to assume, were necessarily rather heavy, Desmond was self-supporting, and his sojourn in Western Australia did not cost the organisation anything.—(Breslin's Official Report, New York, 20 August 1876).

Breslin remained in Sacramento four weeks waiting for funds for his journey, and during this time he received one hundred dollars a week from Talbot for current and future expenses.

Things were not going smoothly in New York. Just as the Rescue Committee were sending Breslin off, Richardson sent in more bills in connection with the vessel. The Treasurer, Patrick Mahon, a business man to the finger tips, refused to pay them until he had examined them and heard explanations. After scrutinising them and hearing the explanations he was perfectly satisfied and paid the bills. A note which Richardson had given Devoy, instead of a receipt, for the first instalment of the price of the *Catalpa* was retained in his own possession by a member of an auditing committee and that created a bad problem for a while. The result was that Breslin had to be kept waiting idly in California for want of funds to enable himself and Desmond to start.

From Sacramento Breslin went to Los Angeles to see John Kenealy and obtained from him all the information he could about Western Australia. He was back in San Francisco by 10 September and was relieved to find amongst his correspondence a notice that funds for his journey had arrived at the telegraph office. Because he was unknown in the city he had great difficulty in getting his money at the telegraph office and was able to do so in the end only through the good offices of Judge M. Cooney, a Clan na Gael man widely known and respected.

All was now ready and Breslin lost no time. On Saturday, 11 September he booked for Desmond and himself a passage by steamer to Australia and changed his dollar bills into gold. The two men spent Sunday with M. W. Stackpoole and some other friends and on the morning of Monday, 13 September they set sail, with Sydney their immediate destination. After a sea journey of more than a month, they landed there on 15 October 1875. On arrival they made enquiry for a trusted man of the Irish Republican Brotherhood, named John Edward Kelly, who had formerly been a prisoner at Fremantle. Kelly deserves a special niche in I.R.B. history. Born in Kinsale, he had gone to the States early, joined the Republican movement there, returned to Ireland to take part in the Fenian rising of 1867, fought at Kilclooney wood in east Cork, was captured and sentenced to be hanged, drawn and quartered. The sentence was commuted to penal servitude, and Kelly had been released in the 1871 amnesty, his health undermined, his spirit and resolve indomitable. He is one of the many staunch Protestant pioneers of Irish liberty. At this time he was running a paper with John Flood. Kelly introduced Breslin and Desmond to two more I.R.B. men of Sydney, whose co-operation in the rescue scheme he considered necessary. One of these was John King. On being introduced to King, Breslin came up against the surprising knowledge that another rescue project was in the course of being planned. John King had left Ireland and gone to Australia after the collapse of the Fenian movement. He set up in the grocery business for a while in Sydney, after which he went to work in the goldfields, where he spent seven years. The rescue plan with which he was connected is best told by himself:

> During all this time I was actively engaged in building up an organisation among Irishmen with the idea of doing something for the release of the prisoners at Fremantle. This was the thought that was ever present in the hearts of Irishmen out there and they responded willingly to efforts on my part and contributed liberally towards a fund which was to be used for that purpose whenever the opportunity might arise. And we had a plan of rescue of our own out there. Our plan was to charter a steamer, man her with our own men, go to Fremantle, rescue the prisoners and take them to the French convict settlement at New Caledonia. We thought we would be well treated there, for only a short time previously Rochefort and three other French newspaper men who were serving a sentence for communism had escaped from New Caledonia and come to Sydney, going from there to England. We had quite an amount of money at our command and all we were waiting for was the proper time to make the attempt at rescue.—(John King's Narrative, *Passaic Sunday Chronicle*, reprinted *Gaelic American*, 8 October 1904).

Kelly was associated with King in this rescue project. Before Breslin's arrival King was engaged in collecting into one central fund all the money which had been contributed by friends in the different colonies. The treasurer of this fund was James McInerney, whose brother owned and operated a stone quarry at Petersham near Sydney. King returned to Sydney and as a help to covering his movements took work as a labourer in the quarries. One afternoon as he and James McInerney were going back into Sydney by bus King noticed Kelly on top of the outbound bus as it approached them.

> There were strangers with him and he signalled to us to get down. We all left the buses and sat down in the shade of a tree by the roadside. Then Kelly introduced me to the stranger and for the first time I had the pleasure of shaking John Breslin by the hand. He was travelling under the name of Collins . . . We had a long talk there together and Breslin seemed very much surprised that we had been active and had a plan of escape under consideration. He showed us that his plan was the best and urged upon us strongly the necessity of absolute secrecy. Desmond was with him. He was known as Mr. Johnston. Breslin was supposed to be looking for an opening in the country to settle there. Outwardly they were utter strangers to each other.—(King's Narrative, *ibid.*).

Breslin told them all the details of the Clan na Gael plan and there and then King, Kelly and McInerney decided to co-operate with Breslin and place all the funds and resources they had at his disposal. Michael Cody, the head of the I.R.B. in Australia, was away in Queensland and Breslin wired for him to come to Sydney. He arranged that Cody should travel through New Zealand, collect from the various I.R.B. branches there the money which had been set aside for the rescue and bring it back, as it would be needed in Fremantle. Breslin's 1876 report describing the rescue suppresses the names of all the Australian I.R.B. men who participated in the scheme, and uses letters of the alphabet to denote persons, a caution induced by fear of retaliation. King, writing many years later, follows his example as regards men still alive in Australia.

Tom Desmond, travelling by the name of Johnston, left for Melbourne on 19 October. Breslin remained on in

Sydney to receive funds, more immediately accessible, promised him by King and A (probably McInerney). The following week he received two hundred pounds from A and out of this he returned thirty pounds to pay the expenses of Michael Cody to New Zealand. Fenian influences were very active in New Zealand. Some years before this there had been intense excitement when Father W. J. Larkin and John Manning, of Hokitika, editors of the *New Zealand Celt,* were imprisoned for alleged sedition and a memorial cross to the Manchester Martyrs in Hokitika cemetery was removed by the police. Cody travelled to New Zealand, where he fulfilled his mission well, and after covering many thousands of miles by steamer and on horseback, returned with between six and seven thousand dollars in gold, which the Irish miners of New Zealand had cheerfully given without asking questions, in the knowledge that it would be used for an important project. It was arranged that King was to bring these funds to Fremantle as soon as they arrived from New Zealand.

Breslin left Sydney on 26 October and arrived in Melbourne on the 30th. Here he visited C and other friends—"friends" in this context always being I.R.B. men. On 4 November he and Desmond took ship from Melbourne for the port of Albany in King George's sound, arriving there on 13 November. The steamer *Georgette,* which made the trip from Fremantle to Albany and back once a month, took them on the last stage of their journey to the city of their assignment. They landed in Fremantle on 16 November.

The following day Breslin rode to Perth, twelve miles away, to take stock of his surroundings, but finding Fremantle the best centre for his proposed operations he made it his headquarters. As James Collins he put up at the Emerald Isle Hotel, the proprietor of which was Patrick Maloney, formerly of County Clare, Ireland. It was the best hotel in town. Desmond went to Perth and got employment at once in a carriage factory where he became known as "The Yankee."

Before leaving San Francisco, Judge Cooney drew up a

legal document which he gave to Breslin. Anyone reading it would conclude that James Collins had large interests in mines and lands in Nevada and other parts of the United States. Breslin left it in his room in the Emerald Isle Hotel, not so carefully concealed as that it would escape the attention of prying eyes, and presently he found that he was being respected in the territory as a millionaire. His actual cost of living and style was, however, below those of an ordinary commercial traveller.

CHAPTER FIFTEEN

THE VOYAGE OF THE *CATALPA*

THE *Catalpa* sailed south. Captain Anthony set about his business as if he were on a normal whaling cruise and did not have any secret locked up in his mind. Everyone on the ship carried out his allotted task and soon they were so busy in pursuit of whales that, for all the crew of the ship knew, nothing else mattered. Items of news about the vessel's progress came to Devoy from time to time. The first was contained in a cutting from the *New Bedford Standard* of 15 June, which Captain Hathaway enclosed with a letter. It ran:

> Brig *Florence*, of Annapolis, N.S., with salt, arrived at St. Stephen yesterday, 63 days from Liverpool. May 10th a violent gale carried away her foremast, main top mast, and all the sails but her main staysail. The provisions ran short, and the vessel drifted helplessly about for 20 days, and crew suffering intensely from hunger and thirst. May 30th bark *Catalpa*, Anthony of this port, rendered assistance and jurymasts were rigged, enabling the vessel to reach the mouth of the St. Croix. During the gale a French sailor named Le Blanc was fatally injured by falling from aloft.

Captain Hathaway's letter, which accompanied this, read as follows:

New Bedford,
June 15th 1875.

To John Devoy, Esq.,
New York.

Dear Friend:

I see by to-night's *Standard* that the *Catalpa* was seen May 30th and rendered assistance to an English brig. I think we will have letters from Capt. A. in a few days. I recd. your dispatch yesterday and am glad to know that everything is settled right . . .

Yours in haste,
A. C. Hathaway.

Two days later he got another letter from Hathaway.

New Bedford,
June 17th 1875.

To John Devoy, Esq.,
New York.

Dear Friend:

Mr. R. received a short letter from Capt. A. dated May 8th, nine days from home. Boiling a sperm whale. Seven days from home he saw whales and killed four of them, but owing to the rough weather they only succeeded in saving but one of them. A. did not write how much oil the whale would probably yield as he wrote but a few lines in haste to send by passing ship. In all probability we will get letters from him in a few days, as he must have sent letters by the ship he supplied provisions to on the 30th May. This is a first rate commencement and I am glad to hear of it so early in the voyage, as it will keep the officers and crew in good spirits. Capt. A. writes that he is very much pleased with the ship and crew. Well he might be, for we were very particular in shipping good men and having things as near right as possible on shipboard. I think this voyage will be a success for all concerned. I have great faith in Captain A., he being a young man who is looking ahead.

Mr. R. received a letter from Reynolds last night dated June 14th, stating he would send the balance of the money in a day or two. I am glad that this part of the job is drawing to a close; it will take a big load from my mind.

I will now close, hoping to hear from you soon.

Yours truly,
Henry C. Hathaway.

Towards mid-August came further news in a letter from John T. Richardson to James Reynolds:

New Bedford,
August 11th 1875.

Friend Reynolds:

I have just received a letter from Capt. Anthony, dated June the 29th. He has taken 110 lbs. of sperm oil (one hundred and ten pounds). He likes his ship first rate, and his crew. He thinks he will get a big catch this season. I should have sent you a letter before this time, but I had no news to send you before this time. If I should receive any more I will let you know.

Your true friend,
J. T. Richardson.

So things went, with letters coming occasionally from Richardson, Hathaway and John Boyle O'Reilly. Reports also came from John J. Breslin, who wrote under the name of James Collins, about his progress right up till the last moment, so that Devoy was kept informed, as fully as circumstances permitted, about the progress of the plans.

Captain Hathaway's opinion that death or casualties were a normal occurrence on a whaling cruise was verified soon enough. During the pursuit of a whale the Kanaka boatsteerer sustained injuries from which he later died. The first mate, Samuel Smith, was also injured but insisted on carrying on under handicap with a perseverance which convinced Captain Anthony that his choice of first mate was a good one. On 14 October Flores was sighted and the chronometer was found to be 120 miles out of reckoning. Towards the end of October the *Catalpa* anchored off Fayal. The catch of oil was landed and consigned to New Bedford. It amounted to 200 barrels, value 12,000 dollars. (*The Irishman,* 9 September 1876). Correspondence for the Captain included letters from his family and a photograph of his baby daughter. Crew trouble arose here. Some of the men deserted and a runner was sent to collect new hands. These men did not have passports and had to be smuggled aboard. A chronometer, to replace the faulty one he had, cost Captain Anthony $110.

Thomas Brennan turned up at Fayal, as instructed, with the intention of joining the ship. He did not succeed. Captain Anthony had got into some trouble at Fayal over an attempt to smuggle American tobacco and had left for St. Michael's before Brennan's arrival. In any case the Captain had made up his mind not to take Brennan on board. In this he was using the discretionary power given him by the Rescue Committee. Besides, he had his own shrewd idea that

Brennan might not work in well. Brennan was severely disappointed. With remarkable tenacity, however, he decided that he must have a part in the rescue and, financed by Goff, Miles O'Brien and Denis Burns, all critics of Devoy, he continued his journey to Australia and arrived there just in time to participate in the rescue. He ever afterwards harboured a strong resentment against Devoy because he concluded, quite wrongly, that the whole thing was a dishonest arrangement of his making.

Captain Anthony cleared his vessel for Teneriffe in the Canary islands. He decided that he must now tell Smith the real purpose of the cruise. After leaving Teneriffe there would be a long weary voyage around the Cape of Good Hope and across the Indian Ocean with no pretence of whaling. Smith must therefore be admitted into the secret before reaching Teneriffe, whatever his reaction. If he refused to assist the enterprise, he must be landed there. Accordingly, when they were a few days out from St. Michael's, Captain Anthony asked Smith to his cabin. He came to the point at once:

> Mr. Smith, you shipped to go whaling. I want to tell you now, before we get to Teneriffe, that the *Catalpa* has done about all the whaling she will do this fall. We're bound to the western coast of Australia to try and liberate six Fenian prisoners who are serving a life sentence in Great Britain's penal colony. This ship was bought for that purpose and fitted for that purpose, and you have been utterly deceived in the object of this voyage. You have a right to be indignant and leave the vessel at Teneriffe. You will have the opportunity when we arrive there, and if you go I can't blame you.
>
> But this ship is going to Australia if I live, and I hope you will stay by me and go with me. God knows I need you, and I give you my word I will stand by you as never one man stood by another, if you will say you will remain in the ship and assist me in carrying out the plans.—(Z. W. Pease: *The Catalpa Expedition*, page 94).

Smith's face was a picture of astonishment at the news. He asked the captain some questions about the men to be rescued, the details of the plan and the organisation behind it. After a brief spell of thought he replied with salty vigour:

"Captain Anthony, I'll stick by you in this ship if she goes to hell and burns off her jib boom."—(*ibid.* page 95). They shook hands warmly. Captain Anthony went to sleep that night a much relieved man.

At Teneriffe he had an awkward time explaining to the consul a discrepancy about the number of the crew, which was given on the ship's papers as 25 but in reality was 22. The position arose out of the trouble at Fayal when he had to ship men without passports. It was an occasion which required all the captain's tact, and for fear the crew would desert again he did not permit any of them ashore but invited the consul on board to regularise matters. He left Teneriffe on 25 November, having taken on board some timber and other materials to build quarters for the rescued men. He told the crew that the material was required for mending the boats, and the explanation was accepted. At Teneriffe, the ship's destination was given as "River la Platte and other places" but from now on the real course lay direct for Western Australia. On 13 December, three small whales were taken, making forty barrels of oil. The *Catalpa* crossed the Equator on Christmas night in Longitude 27 degrees. Two months' monotonous voyaging followed. On 11 February a heavy storm ripped a sail to shreds. The *Catalpa* fell in with the *Platina* of New Bedford, whose captain, Walter Howland, was an intimate friend of Anthony's. But Captain Anthony was not too well pleased to meet him here and had the greatest of trouble in parrying and avoiding his colleague's questions. "Say now, honest, what are you doing here?" On 16 February they fell in with the *Ocean Beauty,* seventy days out from Liverpool. Captain Anthony was looking for a chart of the Australian coast and went on board. The captain was a jolly, communicative Englishman, who knew this part of the world well. In the course of conversation he said he commanded the convict ship *Hougoumont* on its voyage with a shipful of prisoners to Australia in 1868. Not by the flicker of an eyelid did Anthony reveal his astonishment. He asked could the captain spare a chart of the Australian coast. With pleasure, said the captain, and he gave Anthony one which he had used on the *Hougoumont*, showing the west Australian coast in great detail. Pleased at this stroke of luck, Captain Anthony on returning to his ship, related to Smith how, by an almost unbelievable coincidence, he had got the chart of the very vessel which transported the prisoners they were sailing to rescue.

Bad weather delayed the progress of the *Catalpa*. By 15 March, when they sighted the island of St. Paul, they were long overdue in Bunbury. In Fremantle, Breslin was getting worried. Judge Cooney of San Francisco received a letter from one of the Clan na Gael men at Fremantle, expressing anxiety about the non-arrival of the *Catalpa*. The Fremantle correspondent asked Cooney to communicate with New York to know if they had any news of the vessel there.

> Every day now is a day lost, and we will not adopt any other course until we hear from you or until we are satisfied that he will not come; hence we hope you will write to our New York correspondent with the greatest dispatch and let them say whether they will keep their part of the contract and whether Anthony (the vessel) will come or not.—(*Devoy's Post Bag*, I, 172).

This letter was dated 26 March 1876. Two days later the *Catalpa* dropped anchor in Bunbury Harbour. She had been voyaging eleven months, a period of great strain and worry for Captain Anthony.

CHAPTER SIXTEEN

BRESLIN LAYS HIS PLANS

JOHN J. BRESLIN, alias James Collins, was hardly a week in Fremantle when he learned that William Foley was at large in the town. Foley, a native of Waterford, was described by John Devoy as

> one of our best and most faithful Fenian men in the English army.—(*Recollections*, page 157).

He had served part of his sentence in Fremantle prison,

had fallen into poor health, and was now on ticket of leave with a heart impaired by disease contracted in prison. He had access to the prison and to his fellow prisoners, and now became the medium of communication between Breslin and James Wilson. To Wilson he brought the cheering message that Breslin had arrived to lay plans for a rescue which would be organised down to the last detail. Breslin made use of Foley to arrange his method of communication with the prisoners.

By good fortune the prisoners were all located in Fremantle at the time. Towards the end of spring the previous year, all the prisoners not on ticket of leave were sent in from the various gangs in the bush and lodged in Fremantle prison. They were all, except Wilson, engaged in building a reservoir to supply water to shipping in the harbour. Wilson was training a horse for the prison doctor, and this employment gave him a chance of going out of the prison several times a day. In this way he was able to keep in touch more easily with Foley and Breslin. Breslin seized every opportunity of making himself acquainted with the prison lay-out and organisation. While saying nothing about himself, he managed to convey to the residents of Fremantle that he was a wealthy American whose business in the colony was partly pleasure and partly investment. His good manners and attractive personality made him popular with all. Because of his supposed wealth, he gained access to such high society as there was in Fremantle. His social position offered him many advantages, one of the most useful being an invitation, about mid-December, to inspect the convict establishment. Along with two other gentlemen, he was shown through the interior by the Superintendent, Mr. Doonan, whom he had met socially. They inspected all the corridors, the two chapels, the punishment cells, hospitals, cookhouse, workshops and store-room. It was an instructive tour but did not serve to make Breslin over-optimistic. He described the prison as "very secure and well-guarded."

By 1 January 1876, Breslin had had several talks with James Wilson and had determined the plan of escape.

William Foley, in an interview with the *New York Herald*, refers to a lost opportunity of escape, about which details are lacking, but which might have occurred in the first fortnight of January 1876.

> Many disappointments occurred owing to unforeseen accidents, and the golden opportunity was lost through failure to connect with a certain ship. The ability of the agents was tested to the utmost, and the patience of the expectant prisoners was sorely tried.

Foley's term of imprisonment had by now fully expired, his liaison work had been successfully accomplished and, as his health was getting no better, Breslin decided to send him back to New York with the assurance that the escape would be successful. Two days before leaving, Foley had an interview with Wilson. Wilson said to him: "Don't write to us any more, I am confident we shall all follow you soon." He left on 16 January and arrived in New York in mid-July, having travelled by way of London and Ireland. The heart disease he had contracted in prison overcame him shortly after and he died in St. Vincent's hospital, Staten Island.

Breslin did not expect the *Catalpa* to arrive at Bunbury before the end of January. People in Fremantle were beginning to wonder why he remained there so long without any obvious reason, so in order to allay any suspicions he decided to take a trip through the interior of the country as if bound on genuine business. He visited Perth, Guildford, York, Northam, Newcastle and the other smaller villages on that route. Still the *Catalpa* had not come. January, February and March of 1876 passed by and there was no sign of her. Little wonder that Breslin got uneasy. The men he had come to rescue had been shifted around, communication with them had become difficult and they could not be very easily found when wanted.

The prisoners marked time with patience and hope, which they must have found hard enough to sustain at times. Yet there is a barely discernible hint of expectancy in the letter which Martin Hogan addressed to his father, William Hogan, 6 Barrington Street, Limerick, with its promise to "write a longer letter next time."

Fremantle Prison,
Western Australia,
17th March 1876.

My Dearest Father,

I received your letter of November which gave me some comfort to hear from you and I am so happy to hear that you enjoy your health. You say, dear father, write every mail, if possible. I am not able to do that. I will do my best to write every two months. Months and days pass away from me in my long suffering that often I wish to Heaven that the day I received sentence of life that it was death. It would keep me out of long years of misery. Dear Father, you ask me did I get the ticket of leave. I will not for some years to come. Dear Father, send me nothing, no matter what kind it may be. Anything my dear mother has left me keep it till I get it in my own hands. Keep good heart, dear father, I will write a long letter next time.

Your fond son,
Martin J. Hogan.

Write soon.

Martin Hogan's father received this letter on 15 June. By then his son was a free man on the high seas to America.—(*United Irishman*, Liverpool, 1 July 1876).

When an American whaler, the *Canton,* put in at Bunbury, Breslin, inwardly fretting with impatience, telegraphed her captain to know if he had any news of the *Catalpa.* He had none. With time passing, Breslin was beginning to feel really anxious. He decided to go to Bunbury and wait there for some time. He let it be known in Fremantle that he wanted to see that part of the country lying between Perth and the Vasse. On 5 March he booked a seat for the next morning on the mail car to Bunbury. That same day John King arrived in Fremantle by the steamer *Georgette* with £384 (in gold) from the organisers in New Zealand. Breslin gave him back £20 so that he could return to Sydney if he wished, but expressed a preference that he should remain, so as to assist in the rescue. King, only too eager to accept the proposition, stayed on in Fremantle, under the name of Jones, and played an essential part in the rescue scheme. In Fremantle he was supposed to be a gold miner who had come to the colony on the reports of gold having been discovered in the north-west.

Since leaving Sydney, King had had an exciting time enough. He travelled by the P. & O. steamer *China* from Melbourne to Albany, where he was to connect with the steamer *Georgette*. It made the trip to and from Fremantle once a month and was anchored in the harbour. On reaching Albany all the passengers of the *China* and another vessel in port were quarantined on Rabbit Island, because there had been an outbreak of measles in Melbourne when the *China* left and a smallpox case was discovered on the other vessel. The authorities did not know how long quarantine would last. King was in a fix, because if he did not sail by the *Georgette* he would be held up a month. To add to his troubles he got a telegram from Breslin urging haste. He made up his mind that nothing must stop him. With two others he slipped quarantine at night, and rowed in a whale-boat across the harbour to the Fremantle-bound steamer. One of his companions knew the captain well, and they had no difficulty in getting aboard. The money he brought with him was needed because the long delay kept adding to the expenses.

On Monday, 6 March, Breslin travelled by mail coach to Bunbury, 120 miles to the south. He remained there until the following Saturday and, as there was still no tidings of the *Catalpa*, he returned to Fremantle by the little coasting vessel *May*. It was becoming increasingly difficult to give his presence about Fremantle a bona fide appearance. All along his ingenuity got plenty to exercise it in throwing out skilfully veiled hints which were designed to conceal the real purpose of his prolonged stay. Since there was gold in the colony, he talked about gold, and people thought he had a view to prospecting for it. Next he was supposed to be interested in sheep farming, and this notion kept the inquisitive ones occupied for another while. Then he began to talk about timber production, and since a local firm had failed in that business it was thought he was eager to venture on it himself. When that subject had had its innings, Mr. James Collins began to talk wool. One of the most important of the colony's products was wool, which had to be shipped to

England and sold there before the producers could get paid for it. Mr. Collins considered this a thoroughly bad arrangement. Why, he asked, hadn't somebody thought of going round to collect the wool, paying the farmers in cash, and shipping the wool to the best markets available? Naturally, people thought he was going into the wool business. So they kept speculating, and he, by specious turns of conversation, encouraged them to think on harmless lines. His performance was masterly. He kept on the move all the time under pretence of business. Occasionally he travelled to Perth where Tom Desmond, "The Yankee," had been working away constantly at his trade with an employer named Sloan. Desmond, in turn, paid return visits to Breslin in Fremantle.

CHAPTER SEVENTEEN

ENTER WALSH AND McCARTHY

KING'S usefulness was now proved by a novel development. A short time after his arrival Breslin told him he was worried about the appearance of two men in Fremantle, who had come on a sailing vessel from Albany.

> He (Breslin) said that he was afraid they were spies sent out by the English government, as he had learned from the prisoners that two men were expected from England to take an active part in a plan of rescue which had been formulated by patriotic Irishmen over there. Breslin was suspicious that these were the two men in question, and he was afraid of them, because if the government had any inkling of what was going on that would be just what they would do in order to get hold of the ringleaders—send out a couple of spies in the guise of friends to assist in this escape.—(King's narrative, *Gaelic American*, 15 October 1904).

The wary Breslin was sceptical and anxious. He had information that the two men were Denis Florence McCarthy of Cork, and John Walsh of Durham, England, and that they were members of the I.R.B. Still he would take no chances with them. Then King told him he would find out all about them. He told Breslin about two men whose acquaintance he had made on Rabbit Island and whose description fitted

Walsh and McCarthy. King pointed out to Breslin that if these two men were spies it would be better if he, King, were made a scapegoat, so that the leaders of the plan of escape might remain free. He accordingly proposed to make himself known to the two strangers as the leader of the rescue project. If they turned out to be false men the worst that could happen was that King would be thrown into prison. Breslin finally agreed to this plan.

> With this object in view I started out in the evening to meet these men. Fremantle is a small city, nearly all of the inhabitants being convicts—ticket of leave men, as they call them. There are few free men there. These convicts all remain under prison discipline, and when the curfew bell rings at ten minutes to nine they are all obliged to be in their houses for the night. This leaves the streets comparatively deserted after this hour. I was strolling up the principal street when I met McCarthy. He was travelling under the name of Dixon, and I at once recognised him as one of the men I had seen in quarantine on Rabbit Island. I spoke to him and called his attention to the fact that we had met only a short time before and stated the circumstances. He did not remember me at first, or at least he pretended not to. We strolled along talking on various subjects until we reached the outskirts of the city.—(King's narrative, *Gaelic American*, 15 October 1904).

Suddenly King turned to his companion and asked him directly what was he doing in Fremantle. McCarthy, taken aback, said he had an uncle in Champion bay and that he was going there in a few days to assist him sheep raising. King let this pass for a minute and then told McCarthy straight out that he knew all about his plans and his purpose in Australia. McCarthy was astonished and said King was talking downright nonsense. King insisted, however, and told McCarthy all about his proposed plan, the details of which had been given him by Breslin. He added that he was heartily in sympathy with the project and was ready to help materially in it if McCarthy could only convince him that he was genuine. McCarthy hesitated and at last said he would meet King on the beach in half an hour and tell him his decision.

King guessed that he wanted to tell Walsh all about their interview. He was not by any means sure whether they would turn up as friends or with a detachment of police. If his worst suspicions were realised, better to be arrested, for then Breslin would be free to carry on. King went back to the hotel and told Breslin what he had done. Breslin approved and told King to use his own judgment as to whether these two men were to be taken into the confidence of the rescue group. King went to the beach and met McCarthy at the appointed time. McCarthy said he had decided to accept King's offer of help and showed King some documents which proved that he was really acting as agent for the I.R.B. of England and Ireland in a plan to liberate the Fremantle prisoners. King was now fully convinced that McCarthy was "all right" (an I.R.B. password) so he took him down to the Emerald Isle Hotel and introduced him to Breslin.

There we talked matters over. McCarthy stated his plans, which were somewhat similar to ours, but when he found that we had all arrangements perfected he at once volunteered the services of himself and Walsh. They also insisted on turning over a large sum of money, about $5,000, which they had in their possession and which had been contributed by friends to aid in the proposed escape. We declined their money but took their revolvers. Their offer of assistance was accepted and to them was given the task of cutting the telegraph wires on the day of escape. This was all there was for them to do, as every other contingency had been provided for and there was a constant danger in the presence in Fremantle of so many strangers.—*(ibid.)*.

Thus by a remarkable combination of events, three independent movements for rescue, planned in widely separated parts of the world and without previous contact with each other, were canalised into one at the same time and place. The arrival in Australia of Walsh and McCarthy had come about as a result of letters written by the Fremantle prisoners to friends in Ireland and England, calling for a rescue effort. In 1874, when the rescue preparations were in progress in the United States, an envoy of the I.R.B. arrived from Ireland on a business mission to the American organisation. Devoy refers to this envoy with considerable dislike. While in America he was told about the rescue plan, since in his position he had a right to know of it. After his return to

Ireland preparations were made for an Irish-based rescue effort in response to appeals to Ireland and England by the Fremantle captives. This envoy, though cognisant of the American plan, told the home organisation nothing about it and actually encouraged the independent Irish plan of rescue. It was a deliberate suppression of vital knowledge which could have caused untold harm. The envoy might have been "Long John" O'Connor, who did visit the States on I.R.B. business in 1874 and afterwards fell foul of the organisation. Devoy describes an interview he had with him that year, but he does not mention his name in connection with the Australian rescue project. One thing it made clear to the American and home organisations was the necessity for a common scheme of action, and this was very soon afterwards negotiated.

Two notable subscribers to the I.R.B. rescue fund were Joseph Biggar, who contributed £100 as a *loan*, and Joseph Ronayne, who donated £50. The thrifty and affluent Biggar was later repaid his subscription. McCarthy's companion in the venture, John Stephen Walsh, a powerfully built six-footer, was a native of Milford, Co. Cork, but at a later stage of high drama in Irish history he became better known as "John Walsh of Middlesbrough." The I.R.B. was firmly established in Tyneside in those years, and the traditions survived there to such an extent that on the eve of the 1916 rising Newcastle-on-Tyne was still one of the strongest centres of the organisation in Great Britain. John Walsh of Middlesbrough was supposed to be a member of the Invincible group who assassinated Lord Frederick Cavendish and Under-Secretary Burke in the Phoenix Park in 1882. His timely escape to France probably saved him from the fate of Joe Brady and four other Invincibles. All this was in the unknown future.

John King tells us it was only a few days after the inclusion of McCarthy and Walsh in Breslin's rescue plan that a notice appeared on the bulletin board at Fremantle telegraph office saying the *Catalpa* had put in at Bunbury. It put an end to their long anxiety about the ship.

CHAPTER EIGHTEEN

H. M. S. *CONFLICT*

BRESLIN was an early riser. At 6.30 a.m. on the morning of 29 March 1876 he saw on the telegraph bulletin board that the *Catalpa* had put into Bunbury the day before, 28 March. It was a mighty relief. As soon as the office opened at 10 a.m. he telegraphed Captain Anthony:

"Any news from New Bedford? When can you come to Fremantle?"

In the afternoon an answer came:

"No news from New Bedford. Shall not come to Fremantle."

Breslin decided to lose no time now but to carry out the rescue as soon as possible. He immediately engaged a seat on the mail car for Bunbury, set out next morning and arrived there at four in the afternoon. Having put up at the same hotel as Captain Anthony he was introduced to him quite naturally, by a third party, as a stranger. The Captain took the opportunity of inviting him on board the *Catalpa* and there they both discussed their plans without interruption. Breslin explained to the Captain what he wanted him to do with the ship. Captain Anthony was willing to follow any instructions given, but he was handicapped a good deal by crew trouble. The crew thought it strange in the course of the voyage that no effort was being made to pick up whales, and as they were ignorant of the real mission of the ship they became discontented. On the ship's arrival at Bunbury four of them had forcibly taken a boat, rowed ashore at night and escaped into the bush. They were recaptured. Three of them were put in irons on board the ship and the ringleader was closeted in the Bunbury lock-up.

Breslin outlined his plan. He had selected Rockingham beach, twenty miles south of Fremantle, as the most suitable place for embarking the prisoners. It was situated at the head of the sound, and a narrow passage at the end of Garden Island led out to sea. Breslin's scheme was that the *Catalpa* should stand well out to sea, ten or twelve miles outside Garden Island, put a whaleboat into Rockingham beach, collect the rescued men there and pull back out to the ship, a distance of fourteen or sixteen miles, which in ordinary circumstances could easily be done in four or five hours.

Breslin wanted Captain Anthony to see the coast outside of Rockingham and know exactly where his ship should be, so they decided to sail to Fremantle by the coastal steamer *Georgette,* which was coming from Albany and was due in Bunbury on Saturday, 1 April, with the colonial mails. Breslin proposed to carry out the rescue on the morning of Thursday, 6 April. By this arrangement the Captain would have an opportunity to reconnoitre the coast, note the exact spot where Breslin proposed to embark the prisoners, and return to Bunbury in time to clear his ship and bring her north to the position appointed off Garden Island, there to await the arrival of the prisoners. This would also leave Breslin ample time to make the rescue on the morning of 6 April as decided.

The *Georgette* arrived on Saturday and brought a surprise, that was in nowise welcome to Anthony or Breslin, in the person of Thomas Brennan. He had come by a roundabout journey via London to Australia and turned up now, when they had enough responsibility on their hands already. From the deck of the *Georgette* Brennan recognised the *Catalpa* and came ashore to find out what he could do. Breslin already had more men than he could conveniently undertake to provide for, but he had to make the best of things. He could not let Brennan go on board the *Catalpa* at Bunbury without exciting suspicion, so he decided to let him go on to Fremantle and then do the best he could for him by way of assigning him a part in the rescue. Brennan travelled under the name of Hall. On Sunday morning, 2 April, on the way to Fremantle, Captain Anthony, standing on the deck of the *Georgette,* took good stock of the coast outside Rockingham, and noted the positions of Rottnest lighthouse, Garden Island, and other principal features. On sailing into Fremantle harbour they met with a really unpleasant shock.

Anchored there was H.M. gunboat *Conflict*, carrying two guns and thirty men, schooner rigged and fast sailing. She had arrived the previous day and now confronted them with a formidable problem which had not been anticipated.

Breslin and Anthony considered the position in the light of this unexpected hitch. The wind was for the most part light and variable, and the *Catalpa* was a dull sailer unless with a full breeze, so that it would be too dangerous to carry out the rescue and take the slender chance of getting away from the fast-sailing *Conflict*. They decided the rescue could not be effected on Thursday morning nor as long as the *Conflict* remained at Fremantle. On Monday afternoon Breslin, as a result of discreet enquiries, learned that the gunboat had come to Fremantle on an annual visit, would stay eight or nine days and then go either to Adelaide or Sydney. He learned also that another gunboat was expected to call at Fremantle and take Governor Robinson to visit the north-west. This meant some delay and indicated that extreme caution was necessary. Breslin asked Anthony to overhaul and paint the *Catalpa* and be in no hurry to get his wood and water aboard as they must wait until the *Conflict* sailed from Fremantle. He also explained more fully to Captain Anthony the details of the rescue plan and drove him out to Rockingham beach so that he might see and know the spot from which the prisoners were to embark. The drive was also in the nature of a rehearsal to estimate the time it would take to reach the appointed spot. The first ten miles of the road from Fremantle to Rockingham were good for Western Australia. This brought one as far as the Ten Mile Well. From there to Rockingham Hotel, a distance of six miles, it was heavy going, with frequent sandpatches which clogged the wheels and slowed up progress. The last stage, from the hotel to the beach, a distance of four miles, was only a rough track through sand and bush. It took them two hours and twenty minutes to cover the distance, without stopping.

On Thursday, 6 April, Captain Anthony returned to Bunbury. He was to wait there until the *Conflict* left Fremantle and meantime to busy himself with overhauling and painting the *Catalpa.* Before leaving he and Breslin arranged a camouflaged series of telegrams. When the gunboat sailed Breslin would telegraph: "Your friend (N. or S., meaning north or south) has gone home. When do you sail?" This means: "The gunboat has sailed north or south; all right; start for Fremantle." Should the gunboat to take Governor Robinson to the north-west arrive, Breslin would telegraph: "Jones is going overland to Champion bay. When do you clear out of Bunbury?" When the coast was again clear Breslin would send the message: "Jones has gone to Champion bay; did not receive a letter from you." This meant: "All right again."

Five days later, on Tuesday, 11 April, the gunboat *Conflict* sailed out from Fremantle. Breslin learned that she was bound for Sydney. At 10 a.m. he telegraphed Captain Anthony: "Your friend (S.) has gone home. When do you sail?"

Breslin expected Anthony to answer that he would sail that afternoon, in which case the rescue could be carried out on the morning of Thursday, 13 April. Anthony, however, did not reply until Wednesday, 12 April. His message reached Breslin at 11.30 a.m. "I sail to-day. Goodbye. Answer if received. G. Anthony."

This sailing, according to their arrangements, would leave the ship ready to pick up the prisoners on Friday morning. Friday, however, was Good Friday and a government holiday, and the men could not be rescued because the altered prison routine for holidays would not permit it. So Captain Anthony's sailing must be delayed. Breslin telegraphed at once: "Your telegram received. Friday being Good Friday I shall remain in Fremantle and start for York on Saturday morning. I wish you may strike oil. Answer if received."

At half past seven Anthony's reply came: "Yours received. Did not leave to-day. Wind ahead and raining. Sail in the morning. Goodbye."

That fixed the start of operations for Saturday morning, and Breslin made all arrangements for the rescue. Shortly after the *Catalpa* arrived in Bunbury, Breslin, in one of his talks with James Wilson, had arranged a signal he was to make to him which meant "Get ready; we start to-morrow morning." He was unable to give Wilson this signal on Friday, but managed to get a letter through to him on Friday morning, saying the rescue was planned for Saturday morning, giving all necessary instructions and ending with the words: "We have money, arms and clothes; let no man's heart fail him, for this chance can never occur again." News came back to Breslin that Wilson had received the letter.

That Friday evening Tom Desmond came from Perth with a good pair of horses and a four-wheeled wagon. Breslin also had a four-wheeler and had engaged the best pair of horses to be got in Fremantle from Albert's stables, for Friday and Saturday. On Friday afternoon he took the horses out for a drive to make sure they went well together and were in good fettle. On returning to his hotel he found a telegram from Bunbury waiting for him. It said:

James Collins Esq.,

It has blown heavy. Ship dragged both anchors. Can you advance more money if needed? Will telegraph again in the morning.

G. Anthony.

This was a grave disappointment. Things could have been worse, however, and by a rare stroke of luck Robert Cranston had been sent from the prison into town on a message that evening. Breslin had the telegram read to him and his orders of the morning cancelled. Breslin thought that if the ship had dragged both anchors, it must have gone on the bar at Bunbury, and a delay of some weeks might follow before she would be ready for sea again. So he had to send Tom Desmond back to Perth. There was nothing he could do now except wait to see what the next message from Captain Anthony would be. To his great relief, good news came in the morning. At 10.30 a.m. Anthony telegraphed: "I shall certainly sail to-day. Suppose you will leave for York Monday morning. Goodbye. G. Anthony."

Breslin replied at once: "Your telegram received. All

right. Glad you got off without damage. Au revoir. J. Collins."

He then engaged the same horses from Albert's clerk for Sunday and Monday, and sent John King to Perth on a good fast horse which they had bought some months before. King told Desmond to get his team ready and come to Fremantle on Sunday evening. That Saturday afternoon Breslin walked to the jetty at Fremantle, where Wilson and other prisoners were working, and when he was sure Wilson saw him he gave him the signal which meant "We start to-morrow morning." It had slipped Breslin's memory for the moment that the morrow was Sunday. He realised his error when he saw that Wilson looked puzzled, so, keeping him in sight, he walked leisurely across to where the prisoners were working and got close enough to him to say "Monday morning" without attracting the notice of the warder or of any of the other prisoners.

Next day, Easter Sunday, Desmond arrived at Fremantle about two in the afternoon with a very poor looking pair of horses. The pair he had hired previously were not available, having been engaged to go to York as soon as he returned them on Saturday. He offered the hostler five pounds to get him a good pair, but there were none to be had at any price. Breslin then went to get the horses he had engaged for himself and found that Albert had given the best horse of the pair to Mr. Stone, the superintendent of water police, to go to Perth, where his brother-in-law, the sheriff, was in a critical condition as a result of a fall from his horse. Albert also told him that he could not have the horses he had engaged for Monday morning, that his clerk had made a mistake in hiring them to him, as he himself had promised them to Mr. Thompson a week ago, to go to the Perth regatta. Perth regatta was to be held on Easter Monday, the day appointed for the rescue. This regatta was a fortunate diversion, for the officials would all be going there. But it was frustrating about the horses. As things turned out, however, Breslin did not lack a good horse the following morning.

All the men partaking in the morrow's adventure retired

that Easter Sunday night with their minds full of the work before them. King describes how they must have felt:

I don't believe there is a man alive to-day who had anything to do with that escape who will ever be able to forget the terrible anxiety of that Easter Sunday and Monday. We were all fully alive to the desperate chances we were taking . . . You may be sure that we did not get a great deal of sleep that Sunday night. We were all in a state of nervousness for fear that something unforeseen would turn up at the last moment.—(King's narrative, *Gaelic American*, 15 October 1904).

CHAPTER NINETEEN

THE RESCUE

FOR Captain Anthony, too, it was a full and anxious week-end. On the morning of Saturday, 15 April, after receiving the telegram from Breslin confirming the arrangement for Monday morning, he went to the Bunbury custom house to announce he was ready to clear ship for sea. The customs officers came on board and checked every corner of the ship to see that there were no stowaways. That was the custom in the colony. Anchor was hoisted at 2 p.m. and the *Catalpa* sailed out of Bunbury. Favoured by a light breeze she moved slowly north towards Rottnest Island.

By noon on Sunday she was about twenty miles south of Rottnest lighthouse. Anthony called Smith into the cabin, and explained what was to be done. There was to be a radical deviation from the original plan. He was going ashore himself in the whaleboat. In doing this he was taking a grave personal risk and if he were lucky enough to escape capture, his career in the whaling business would be at an end in any case. The circumstances under which he made this self-sacrificing decision are explained by John Devoy:

I had arranged with him that the *Catalpa* was to wait off shore outside the three-mile limit, and the men were to be taken out in boats procured in Australia, so as to keep the captain and the ship from being made amenable to international law. When Captain

Anthony got to Bunbury, however, he at once saw that no boats procurable there would be fit for the work, and that ordinary oarsmen unaccustomed to work in the open sea would be utterly unable to cope with the conditions. He therefore determined to take the men off in the vessel's whaleboats, pulled by his own men, and to take charge of the work himself, regardless of consequences to his seafaring career. The result showed that but for this decision of Captain Anthony the attempt at rescue would have been a total failure.—(*Gaelic American*, 8 October 1904).

Captain Anthony explained to Smith that Rottnest lighthouse, twelve miles offshore from Fremantle jetty, had a signal room on top to warn the town of the approach of any ships. He was therefore to keep well clear of it, but to work the ship on and off some miles outside Garden Island and to keep a sharp lookout for the return of the whaleboat. If things went wrong and Captain Anthony did not come back Smith was to continue whaling or return to New Bedford as he thought best. Samuel Smith, a stalwart Nantucket Islander of Scottish parentage, stands out as one of the most resolute and engaging personalities of the voyage. Although American to the core, his Scottish blood bound him by ties of race to the Irishmen he was helping, and there can be no doubt that he shared their feelings thoroughly. He wished the Captain Godspeed on the dangerous task ahead. They shook hands and said good-bye, with the Captain secure in the knowledge that he was leaving the ship in good hands.

Captain Anthony now selected five of his best crewmen, provisioned the whaleboat, and shoved off. They made sail for Garden Island sound. Towards nightfall the sail was taken down and oars were used. Off the south end of the island the boat was almost miraculously hoisted by huge breakers over a sunken rock and lifted into calm waters. They rowed safely on to the beach, and hauled the boat up the beach. The Captain's sense of direction had been faultless. On their former visit, he and Breslin had driven stakes down in the sand to mark the spot chosen for embarkation. Walking around he stumbled on them about a hundred yards away. It was half-past eight and the night was dry and warm. They had supper, and the men, on the captain's instructions, lay down on the grass and soon went to sleep. Captain Anthony slept little that night.

Easter Monday, 17 April, dawned. Breslin was up early. At half-past five he had the ostler called and the valises put in the trap. Then he awakened King and Desmond. Brennan, already up and dressed, left for Rockingham beach at six o'clock, with a two-wheeled trap filled with luggage. His assignment was to locate Captain Anthony, tell him to expect the others and have everything ready.

At seven o'clock Breslin went to Albert's stables and found the pair of horses he wanted and a nice light four-wheeled trap already harnessed up and waiting. He told the ostler to let them stand for about twenty minutes, and then went to tell Desmond to get his horses harnessed and be ready to start at half-past seven. Everybody was carefully instructed on what to do. Desmond was to leave Fremantle by a side street which, after a few turns, would take him on to the Rockingham road. Breslin was to drive up High Street as if going to Perth, turn sharp round by the prison and get on to the Rockingham road as well. King, who had a fast horse, was to remain behind for a reasonable time after the rescue was effected, then follow to let them know if the alarm had been raised. At half-past seven Breslin rode leisurely up the High Street, turned to the right on reaching the prison, and walked his horses by the warden's quarters and pensioners' barracks.

The men were beginning to assemble for parade. Breslin had arranged with Wilson and the other Fenians that he would have the carriages in position on the road at a quarter to eight, and that they would remain there in readiness for them, with the nearest one standing within five minutes' run of the prison, until nine o'clock. As he was a little early, Breslin drove slowly along the Rockingham road. After a few minutes Desmond drove up behind him and passed him out. At a shaded part of the road they stopped and divided the hats and coats which they had brought for the prisoners placing three of each in each trap. Breslin turned round again and drove slowly back to Fremantle, Desmond following close behind.

It was now five to eight. A few minutes later Breslin, looking in the direction of the prison, saw three men appear some distance ahead. They wheeled round and marched down the Rockingham road towards him. Driving forward, he recognised them as Wilson, Cranston and Harrington. He told them to pass on quickly, get into Desmond's trap and drive away. Desmond wheeled his horses around for Rockingham, the three men got into his carriage without losing a second and off he went at a furious gallop in clouds of dust. Almost immediately three other men appeared from the direction of the prison. Breslin drove towards them. One was carrying a spade and another a large kerosene can. As soon as they recognised Breslin, the man with the spade threw it with a javelin-cast into the bush, and the man with the kerosene can sent it sailing through the air with a resounding drop-kick. They were Darragh, Hogan and Hassett. Breslin now had all the men he wanted and began to wheel his carriage around towards Rockingham. The road was too narrow for such a manoeuvre at this point and the horses reared. Darragh caught one of them by the head to try and lead them round, but it kicked and pranced so vigorously that Breslin feared it would break the harness. He told Darragh to let go, drove the horses on to a wider part of the road where they wheeled round without a hitch, drove back to his men, picked them up and raced hell for leather down the Rockingham road after Desmond, who was now well out of sight.

King had remained behind in the Emerald Isle Hotel to keep his eyes open for any alert which might be given. Passing through the dining room after breakfast, he noticed a large piece of cake on the table and, schoolboy fashion, tucked it under his coat, not knowing but it might be wanted. It was after eight when he mounted his horse and left the hotel. Everything was quiet in the city and he felt the men had been successful in getting away. He rode past the prison, where all was quiet, trotted down the Rockingham road and presently urged his horse to a brisk canter and soon to a full gallop. In a short time he overtook Breslin and reported that all was well and no alarm had so far been raised. Breslin told him to follow and keep five miles in the rear. It was fortunate for the Fenians that the prison arrangements permitted them to have contact and communication with each other. Their good conduct and the length of time they had served entitled each of them to the rank of constable. This enabled them to communicate with each other with greater ease than the other prisoners. Wilson and Harrington had been working in the same party on a harbour building scheme in Fremantle. Hogan was a painter by trade. On the morning of the rescue he was employed painting the house of Mr. Fauntleroy, outside the prison walls. Cranston had a job in the stores and did occasional messenger work. Darragh was a clerk and attendant to the Church of England chaplain and had considerable freedom in communication with the other prisoners. On the morning of the escape he took Hassett with him to plant potatoes in the garden of Mr. Broomhole, the clerk of works.

After breakfast that morning all the prisoners contrived to be engaged outside the walls on one business or another. Cranston passed out as if going on a message, overtook warder Booler, who was in charge of the working party which included Wilson and Harrington, showed him a key, and told him he had been sent to take Wilson and Harrington to move some furniture in the Governor's house. This was the nearest point at which they expected to meet Breslin. The warder obligingly told Wilson and Harrington to go with him. Darragh took Hassett, as if going to work, in the same direction, and was joined by Hogan, who made an excuse to the warder in charge of him and was permitted to go. Both parties of three met the rescuers, exactly as planned, on the Rockingham road.

The dash for Rockingham beach and freedom was now on, Desmond leading, Breslin close behind, and King on horseback taking up the rear, while clouds of fine dust rose in the air behind them. At the Rockingham Hotel they were hailed by Somers, the proprietor, who knew Breslin. He wanted to know what time was the *Georgette* expected at Rockingham jetty. Breslin was inwardly disconcerted at hearing that the *Geor gette* was expected, as this could upset his plans, but outwardly cool as he replied casually that the vessel was at Fremantle jetty when he was leaving and he could not really say.

Some half-dozen miles ahead, on the Rockingham beach, Captain Anthony, astir since daybreak, found himself situated not far from the Rockingham Jarrah timber station. In the course of the morning employees began carting timber to the jetty, half a mile away, and one of them, full of curiosity, came up to Anthony, wanting to know what was going on. Anthony told him he was going to Fremantle for an anchor in place of one which he lost. The man was friendly and said he was an ex-prisoner himself. Captain Anthony held him in conversation, knowing that Breslin's party, if successful, must soon turn up. Very likely this man was Bell, who figures in contemporary Australian accounts as a witness of the rescue, but a description published in the American papers says that the man whom Anthony held in conversation was an old British official (see *The Irishman,* 9 September 1876, which reprints reports from the American papers). He told Anthony in the course of conversation that the *Georgette* was coming to the jetty, and this, naturally, did nothing to ease Anthony's mind.

To add to his uneasiness, he now saw the smoke of the vessel in the distance. But he knew that the arrival of the men could not be long delayed. Nor was it. Soon afterwards Brennan arrived in his two wheeler with the luggage and announced that the others were coming. He was followed, after a brief interval, by King on horseback with a like announcement, and finally Desmond and Breslin raced on to the beach in their four-wheelers with the full complement of rescued men. The carriages and the exhausted, perspiring horses were left on the beach while the men lost no time in making for the whaleboat.

The beach, previously quiet, now became alive with their sudden onset, their brisk movement, their shouts and action. The official whom Anthony had held in talk stared open-mouthed at the scene, while the crew of the whaleboat took alarm at the swift approach of so many men, all of whom were seen to be armed to the teeth. The crew thought it was an attack, but Captain Anthony reassured them. When the party arrived on the beach, "the man Bell" (the phrase is the *Times's*) attached himself to them, and if he is to be identified with the old British official who showed such astonishment at their sudden appearance a moment before, he certainly recovered his presence of mind quickly, and at once became inquisitive about their business. They described themselves to him as excursionists. He attended to the horses and accompanied them to where Captain Anthony, at the water's edge, was waiting with his whaleboat and crew. They told Bell they were going aboard, and one of them gave him a sovereign to drink their health. He asked them what he would do with the horses and traps, and was told shortly to "let them go to hell." Bell looked into one of the traps and saw some convict caps and other suspicious articles. He concluded that the men were convicts and he returned to Fremantle to report what he had seen, using John King's fast saddle-horse which had been abandoned on the spot.

Meantime, rescuers and rescued had lost no time in taking their places in the whaleboat, where they were told to stow themselves into as small a space as possible, so as not to hamper the oarsmen. The boat shoved off and the crew pulled at the oars, badly at first, because they were disconcerted by their fright and the sudden turn of events, but encouraged by Captain Anthony, who told them to pull as if racing after a whale, they soon worked steadily in concert away from Rockingham beach and out towards the open sea. Bell, who had been watching the scene and investigating the carriages, rode back to Fremantle to give the alarm. Before he reached the town the prisoners had been missed, the prison officials were in a panic and there was uproar and almighty confusion. Martin Hogan, who was supposed to be painting the controller's residence, was the first to be missed. A search failed to find him. His absence led to enquiry being made for the other Fenian prisoners. They were found to be missing too. The police were notified and patrols sent out. When Bell rode in, a party of mounted police had only just returned after a fruitless search in the bush. Their next step was to be a search of suspected houses and shipping. John Walsh criticised the way in which things had been managed during the dash to Rockingham. He said that Breslin should have arrested Bell and any other person they met, taken them away in the whaleboat and marooned them on an offshore island, so that they would be powerless to raise the alarm. Had this been done, he argued, their departure via Rockingham beach would not have been discovered as early as it was because, until Bell brought the news, the prison officials had no idea in which direction they had gone. That is Walsh's version, and he certainly was in Fremantle or its neighbourhood at the time, so he would know what happened. As soon as they learned from Bell that the prisoners had escaped in a whaleboat, the authorities tried to telegraph to Albany in King George's sound to warn the *Conflict* to intercept them. But the telegraph wires were cut. Walsh and McCarthy had done their part thoroughly. It took hours of precious time to repair the lines. By the time the message was flashed to King George's sound it was too late. The *Conflict* had left port an hour and a half previously, bound for Adelaide. This was a happy stroke of luck for the rescue expedition. But, insisted Walsh, it was a serious error to have let Bell go.

By the time the mounted police reached Rockingham beach, the whaleboat with the rescued men was several miles off shore. There was nothing the police could do. They found the horses unattended, and in the carriages three prison hats, some revolver cartridges, a breechloading rifle cartridge, a bottle of wine and a woollen gun-cover. It was clear that the rescue party was armed and fully prepared to resist. Looking towards land, the men in the whaleboat could see them round up the horses and traps and drive them slowly up the beach towards the Rockingham jetty. The crew pulled away strongly, steadily, every stroke of the oars bringing them nearer to safety.

In Fremantle there was pandemonium amongst the prison authorities. An eye-witness of the scene which followed the escape writes:

They were not missed for about an hour and a half, and then there was a scene of the wildest excitement, officials running here and there, mounted policemen flying with orders and despatches, and finally two mounted policemen and a native black man, a tracker, followed in pursuit to Rockingham, but the prisoners evidently had too long a start of them and they returned to Fremantle.—(Letter dated Fremantle, 18 April 1876, reprinted *United Irishman*—Liverpool —10 June 1876).

This correspondent heard that the prisoners and their friends were well armed, and the belief in Fremantle was that they would make a desperate resistance and would not be taken alive. It was considered to be one of the most clever and daring schemes of escape ever carried out, and the expectation was "that there will be hard times for the officials and lots of dismissals" as a result. "I need hardly tell you," added the writer, "that the Irish people here are in the very highest state of jubilation at the escape of the prisoners."

Details of the scene at Rockingham beach, given by Bell, included the information that the prisoners had embarked in a whaleboat manned with "six coloured men and another man of Yankee look" (*Fremantle Herald* quoted *United Irishman*—Liverpool—5 August 1876). It was known that the American whaler *Catalpa* had cleared out of Bunbury the Saturday before, and as no other vessel was known to be off the coast, it was concluded that the whaleboat in which the prisoners escaped belonged to that vessel. Arrangements were at once made to go in pursuit. The superintendent of water police sent out the police cutter in charge of coxswain Mills. She left Fremantle at 1.30 p.m. and off Sulphur bay, Garden Island, she spoke to a fishing boat, and was told that a whaleboat had pulled out of the south passage between Perron point and the south end of Garden Island. After clearing the passage the whaleboat had run up a sail and steered south. Following this cue, the police boat coasted along close inshore as far as Murray head which she made at half-past seven. Seeing no sign of the whaleboat, she then steered out to sea under easy sail, keeping a sharp look out. She remained at sea all night but saw nothing and returned to Murray head early next morning.

CHAPTER TWENTY

TOUCH AND GO

Hurrah for the mountain side!
Hurrah for the bivouac!
Hurrah for the heaving tide!
If rocking the felon's track.

—Michael Doheny.

THE whaleboat carried sixteen men. They were, Captain Anthony and his five crewmen, the six rescued men, Breslin, Desmond, King and Brennan.

At half-past twelve they were clear of the reefs to the seaward of Garden Island. They hoisted the boat's sails and steered in a south-easterly direction in search of the *Catalpa.* They held this course until four in the afternoon but saw no sign of her, so they took in the sail and rowed due west. About half-past five Toby, one of the crew, sighted the *Catalpa* about fifteen miles ahead, and the men rowed vigorously to get as near as possible to her before dark. At half-past six they could see her topsails clearly from the crests of the waves. They hoisted a sail to speed their progress and attract the whaler's attention. Bad weather came down. The skies got black and squalls of driving rain soaked them to the skin, but still they made good headway and were gaining on the ship when misfortune struck them. About seven o'clock a vicious squall hit the boat and broke the mast short off at the thwart. By the time they had the mast and sail stowed away, night had fallen and the *Catalpa* had been swallowed up in the darkness. They kept rowing in her direction until ten o'clock, hoping to be able to see her lights, so as to remain in her company, but they saw nothing. They then hoisted the jibsail on an oar and steered the course they thought she had gone.

While the men in the whaleboat were rowing out to sea, the authorities in Fremantle had not been idle. They considered that, because the wind was westerly, the ship assisting in the escape of the prisoners could not work off the shore and might even now be in territorial waters and therefore subject to British jurisdiction. It was decided to place the *Georgette* under commission and send her in pursuit. The consent of the agent, Mr. John McCleery, was obtained, and indemnity was given him in case his ship might be damaged or lost. She was then equipped for pursuit and possible encounter with the *Catalpa*. John Stone, superintendent of water police, was placed in command with instructions to go alongside the *Catalpa* and try to find out whether the prisoners were aboard, and if they were, to demand their surrender, warning the captain of the consequences of his act if he refused to give them up. No force was to be used and the *Georgette* was to be back by noon of next day, Tuesday, if possible. It was nine o'clock before the ship was ready and then the twelve pounder gun had to be left behind. In addition to her usual crew, there were eighteen men of the Enrolled Pensioners force aboard under Major Finerty, and eight policemen, all fully armed. Fremantle was agog with excitement, and the jetty was thronged with people as the *Georgette* set out.

It was a bitterly cold and rainy night. The sea was rough and the weather stormy with no signs of it easing off. Ugly seas threatened to swamp the whaleboat and the men were kept busy baling out. In this dangerous situation Anthony kept the men's spirits up by making small of the hazards and shouting words of encouragement and re-assurance like the great captain that he was. Towards two in the morning it calmed down. At a quarter to seven they sighted the *Catalpa* again and steered towards her. She was coming in their direction and, with her lower sails soon visible, there was every hope they would shortly be on deck, when Breslin, looking behind, saw the smoke of a steamer.

It was the *Georgette*, steaming out from Fremantle with all sail set. She had rounded Rottnest Island in the night and made about thirty miles S.W. of the island by daybreak. Her course was then laid S.E. It was her regular day for sailing to Albany with the colonial mails, and for a short time they were in doubt as to whether she was engaged in pursuit or going on her usual trip. After watching her for a little while they decided she was too far out of her regular course to be going to Albany, and while they still watched her she changed course and made for the *Catalpa*. Captain Anthony now plied oar and sail to reach the *Catalpa* first, but it soon became clear that the *Georgette* was sailing so fast that she would reach the *Catalpa* much sooner than they could. She was also coming uncomfortably close to the whaleboat, so they took down the sail and lay to, hoping that she would pass them by without seeing them. She did pass by and sailed directly towards the *Catalpa*, now five miles away.

When she had gone far enough ahead they pulled in her wake, judging that it was safe to do so if she was looking for them. Also it would bring them nearer the *Catalpa*. They could see the *Georgette* run alongside the *Catalpa*. On board the *Georgette* all preparations had been made for defence, with crew, pensioners and police under arms. The *Catalpa* was flying the Stars and Stripes. In reply to questions from the superintendent of water police, First Mate Smith stated that his captain was at Fremantle, that no boat had been seen, and that he was awaiting the captain's return. In reply to the question: "Can I board your ship and search?" he coolly replied: "Don't know, got no instructions, but guess you'd better not." So runs the *Fremantle Herald* account, but Smith's refusal, it would appear, was delivered with more abrupt vigour in words to the effect that they could not "by a damned sight" come aboard his ship. The *Georgette* remained alongside about ten minutes, but her quest was fruitless. From the whaleboat, Breslin's party could see her steam slowly away while the *Catalpa* held on her course. The *Georgette* veered gradually shorewards and they concluded she was making for Bunbury.

The police cutter had also been searching for the prisoners since early morning, making short tacks to the south as far as Cape Bouvard, and had also sighted the *Catalpa* to the west and while making towards her met the *Georgette* returning. The officer in charge of the *Georgette* reported to them that the escaped prisoners were not on board, that the mate had told him the captain was on shore and that the vessel was waiting for him to come off. He gave instructions to the coxswain in charge to cruise along the coast and keep a sharp look out, as there could be no doubt the ship's boat with the escaped prisoners was concealed somewhere near Murray head. Some time later the *Georgette* headed for Fremantle, as she was running short of coal.

It was now half-past eight a.m. They made a sail again on the whaleboat and put out every oar and paddle available in a determined effort to overtake the *Catalpa.* The ship held on her course, steering S.S.E., and both she and the *Georgette* kept increasing their distances from the whaleboat. About half-past eleven, when the *Catalpa* was about twelve and the *Georgette* eight miles away, they saw the *Georgette* turn right round and head towards Fremantle, working her way along the coast, and by all appearances on the look out for them. She was, in fact, making for Fremantle to re-coal. They were now practically in her track and if she stood out to sea a little she could hardly fail to observe them. However, they pushed doggedly on in the wake of the *Catalpa,* which was still holding the same course and was now receding from sight in the distance. They began to call her "the phantom ship." The *Georgette* was coming perilously near to the whaleboat, so they took down the sail and worked away at the oars. Closer still came the *Georgette,* and they were certain now they would not escape being seen. Captain Anthony told them to stop rowing for a while and to lie as low as they could in the boat, knowing from his long experience of the sea that a boat lying in the wave troughs stood a chance of not being observed from the deck of a nearby vessel. About half-past twelve the *Georgette* passed across their wake so close that they could make out men on her deck and a lookout man at her masthead. Every moment they expected her to turn and make towards them, but miraculously she did not see them, and as soon as her hull sank in the distance they put up their sail again and pulled resolutely on after the *Catalpa.*

They now began to gain slowly on her, and as they did she gradually loomed up larger. About two p.m. they saw that she had altered course and was coming in their direction. Breslin placed Wilson in the bow of the whaleboat, holding aloft a blue flag, and half an hour later they felt certain they were seen from the *Catalpa,* which was now heading straight for them.

Then they saw something else which gave them a shock. It was another boat under sail, also making towards the *Catalpa,* and about the same distance from it on the landward side as they were to seaward. In a few minutes they identified it as the water police cutter. It became a race between them, their object being the *Catalpa,* while the cutter's design was to reach across their course and head them off. Pulling fiercely, they strained every nerve and sinew in a final effort. Thomas Darragh admired the masterly seamanship of Smith in manoeuvring the *Catalpa* in between the two crafts. It was the stroke of victory, for the whaleboat reached the *Catalpa* on the weather side while the police boat was still four hundred yards away on the lee side. Haste was imperative. The *Catalpa's* hoisting tackle was let down to pick up the boat, and the men lost no time in scrambling on board. As soon as Breslin's feet struck the deck he heard Smith call out: "What shall I do now, Mr. Collins?"

Breslin answered: "Hoist the flag and stand out to sea."

Never, said Breslin, describing the moment afterwards, was a manoeuvre executed in a more prompt and seamanlike manner. Within two minutes the Stars and Stripes were flying overhead, the rescue boat was hoisted and secured at the davits, and the ship was turned round and standing on her course out to sea. In that time the police cutter was coming alongside. As the *Catalpa* went past, Breslin, who had a nice sense of the dramatic, stepped to the rails and, as he said, "kissed my hand to the gentlemen who had lost the race." It was certainly a memorable moment for the victors. The *Catalpa* stood on her course and the cutter dropped astern. The official in charge of the cutter, who appeared to be a good humoured man with, who knows, a tinge of admiration for the daring of the escape, called out "Good-bye, Captain, good-bye." This is also stated in the log book of the *Catalpa*, which describes the event in these brief words:

At 2 p.m. wore ship and headed more northward. At 2.15 raised the boat N.N. by E. Kept off for her, and at 3 p.m. she came alongside with eleven* passengers. The coastguard boat was in sight. She hoisted her flag and we hoisted ours, and wore ship. The coastguard boat was alongside of us, and her captain wished us good-bye. (Quoted in *The Irishman*, 9 September 1876).

The version of the encounter given in the Western Australian papers more or less confirms Breslin's account which we have been following. The police boat had been searching the waters continuously, keeping the *Catalpa* within sight all the time. It stood to the southward about two miles to leeward of the whaler until past noon, when the ship tacked and stood to the north. The police boat tacked in keeping with the whaler and soon after saw a whaleboat ahead and to leeward.

Chase was at once given, the police boat gaining fast, when the *Catalpa* bore down under all sail, picked up the whaleboat and stood away. At the time the whaleboat was picked up by the ship she was not more than 400 yards ahead. After picking up the whaleboat, the police boat was to leeward of the ship within twenty yards and saw distinctly the escaped Fenians looking over the bulwarks, some of them in prison dress. A person named "Collins," who had been living in Fremantle for some months past, and who is suspected of being the organiser of the escape, was also recognised. The police boat did not hail the ship nor did the ship hail the boat. The ship stood away south and the police boat returned to Fremantle, which place she reached about ten o'clock that night. The men on board the ship appeared to be armed, and it was quite evident from the behaviour of the escaped prisoners while the police boat was within range, that they were only restrained from firing upon the boat by the influence of the captain.—(*Fremantle Herald*).

The men had been twenty-eight hours in the open boat, drenched with rain and spray, their limbs cramped for want of room, and their hearts tense with the palpitating uncertainty of whether they should gain their freedom or be recaptured for the dreaded chain-gang. They changed clothes and the warmth coursed through their bodies with the revivifying effect

* The whaleboat contained sixteen men.

of glasses of New England rum and steaming hot mugs of coffee. The heroes of the hour were Anthony and Breslin. The rescued men gathered around them to grasp their hands and cheer them with hearts full of joy and gratitude for their deliverance. Anthony's part in the affair had been above all praise. With no ties of race to the rescued men, he had carried out more than his share of the enterprise with rare devotion and courage. He had proved more than true to the testimony given of him by Captain Hathaway:

> The man who engaged to do this will keep that engagement, or he won't come out of the penal colony.—(Roche, *O'Reilly*, page 171).

John King describes the scene on board the *Catalpa*:

> Then the prisoners felt that they were free at last and they gathered around Breslin and fell on the deck and kissed his feet in token of their gratitude. We were all overwhelmed with thanks and it certainly was a relief . . . —(King's narrative, *Gaelic American*, 22 October 1904).

Supper was served and they fell to with a will. After that they walked the deck and watched the shores of Western Australia fading on the horizon. It was their last glimpse of the land of bondage. The *Catalpa* worked to windward, with a light breeze blowing in the direction of Cape Naturaliste. At nine p.m. all hands except the watch on deck retired. They slept soundly after their adventures. But there was further adventure in store.

CHAPTER TWENTY-ONE

'HEAVE TO!'

AFTER her futile trip to the *Catalpa*, the *Georgette* returned to Fremantle. Her coal supply was running short and, besides, the officer in charge was evidently undecided what to do and thought it well to seek further instructions. She reached Fremantle jetty at four o'clock in the afternoon. An excited crowd had gathered, eager to hear what news. Popular opinion was divided. The predominant feeling was a hope that the prisoners had got clear away. When the particulars became known there were some who expressed regret that the *Georgette* had returned without making a more definite effort. People said that if she had stayed out and hovered around the *Catalpa* she could have prevented the prisoners from boarding the ship and made their escape impossible. John Walsh thought so, too, only he wasn't giving the benefit of his opinion. But, states the *Fremantle Herald*,

> the general feeling was clearly one of pleasure that the pursuit had so far been unsuccessful. This arose chiefly out of the popular impression that Fenian convicts are political prisoners, convicted and punished for offences against a government, not against society, and from the sympathy that the public everywhere display towards the weak in a contest against the strong.

This liberal view was not shared by the authorities, as we shall see.

It soon became known to the residents of Fremantle that a second attempt to recapture the escaped men would be made and that his Excellency the Governor was visiting the town personally to give instructions. The town was in a fever of excitement. The local paper describes the scene:

> Alarm, excitement, bustle and activity were exhibited on all hands. Never were the people of Fremantle so upset or so excited. Business was almost entirely suspended and the imposing Masonic ceremony of laying the foundation stone of the new Freemason's hall, which was to take place at four o'clock, was almost forgotten, and attracted but little if any attention. In the course of the afternoon his Excellency, accompanied by the Colonial Secretary, drove down, and after consultation with the superintendent of water police, the comptroller general, and other officials, and the agent for the *Georgette*, it was decided to despatch the *Georgette* again for the *Catalpa*, with a view to intercept the boat, or to demand the surrender of the prisoners from the captain, if they were on board.—(*Fremantle Herald*).

The pensioners and police again manned the ship and this time the twelve pounder field piece, which had been brought all the way from Perth, was put on board and fixed in the gangway, his Excellency himself giving a hand at hoisting it and securing it on deck. The vessel was provisioned and a fatigue party of pensioners shovelled thirty tons of coal on board her in record time. At eleven o'clock that night everything was ready, and the *Georgette* steamed out from the jetty, into the dark night, leaving the excited crowd to their speculations.

Morning, 19 April, dawned, and on board the *Catalpa*, Breslin, sensing that all was not yet over, was on deck at five o'clock, to be on the lookout for any emergency. The *Catalpa's* course had been altered, and she was now steering to windward on a light breeze in a N.N.W. direction. This would bring them past Fremantle again outside Rottnest Island. At 5.30 the man on the lookout reported a sail on the lee bow. The first mate identified her as the *Georgette*. As day brightened they could see her more clearly standing across their course and evidently looking for them. At six o'clock they passed her as she lay half a mile to windward of them. She was flying a man-of-war and vice-admiral's flag. Captain Anthony set the Stars and Stripes as the *Catalpa* passed and held on his course. The *Georgette* turned and followed. A freshening breeze about seven o'clock helped the *Catalpa* and the *Georgette* began to drop astern.

The stokers on the *Georgette* got busy, fired up the furnaces and, powered by steam, she began to overhaul the *Catalpa* quickly. With the breeze dying away, the *Catalpa* was now making little headway. At a quarter to eight the *Georgette* had come so close that Breslin could see she had guns, an artillery unit and the water police on board. A whaleboat belonging to the water police hung at her davits, presumably to be used in boarding, "and," to quote Breslin's report, "they seemed quite eager and determined to capture us." The Fenian party were all in the cabin with rifles and revolvers ready. Nobody was visible to those on the *Georgette* except the lookout and the helmsman. Breslin went below to the cabin and in a few brief words explained the position to the men.

"If the officials on board the Georgette are determined to fight for your recapture," he said, "they will most probably succeed, as they have the advantage of us in every way. They have more men, they are better armed, they have cannon, and a steamer with which they can sail round and round us. Those of us who have not been in prison can only suffer imprisonment, but if any life is lost as a result of our resistance, those of us who have escaped from prison are liable to be hanged. It is simply a case of dying now or of waiting to die in prison. You can choose between fighting, or surrendering if the officials on the *Georgette* fire into us or board us."

The men replied: "We will do whatever you say."

Breslin said: "I will hold out to the last," and went back on deck. The *Georgette* was now close up on the weather side. Breslin saw a company of artillery on board, with a field piece trained on the *Catalpa* and the gunners at their posts. At eight o'clock the *Georgette* steamed ahead and fired a shot across the *Catalpa's* bows. Captain Anthony asked Breslin what he should do. Breslin replied: "Hold on, and don't take any notice of the shot yet."

The artillery men on the *Georgette* reloaded their piece and pointed it straight at the *Catalpa*. The two ships were now sailing side by side, within easy speaking distance, and Breslin told the captain to ask what they wanted. Captain Anthony stepped on the weather rail and raised his speaking trumpet to his lips. As he did so the *Georgette* hailed:

"Bark ahoy!"

"What do you want," asked Captain Anthony.

"Heave to," came the order from the *Georgette*.

"What for," shouted Captain Anthony.

There was a pause. Captain Anthony repeated the question louder.

"What am I to heave to for?"

After a while the *Georgette* hailed: "Have you any convict prisoners aboard?"

"No prisoners here, no prisoners that I know of."

"I telegraphed to your government," said the *Georgette's* spokesman. "Don't you know you are amenable to British law in this colony? You have six convict prisoners on board. I see some of them on deck now."

Breslin told the captain that the *Georgette* spokesman was lying and trying to bluff; he could not send a message to Adelaide before next Saturday.

The *Georgette* hailed again: "I give you fifteen minutes to consider and you must take the consequences; I have the means to do it, and if you don't heave to I'll blow the masts out of you."

Breslin, who took up a position where he could not be seen from the *Georgette*, was standing by to advise the captain what to do. On his instructions, Captain Anthony replied: "That's the American flag. I am on the high seas. My flag protects me. If you fire on this ship you fire on the American flag."

The threat to fire on the flag thoroughly roused the anger of First Mate Samuel Smith, patriotic American that he was, and he drew on his remarkable fund of nautical phrases to call down damnation, by and large, on the man who threatened. "Damn him," he exclaimed, "let him sink us. We'll go down with the ship. I'll never start sheet or tack for him." He asked Breslin what he would do if the *Georgette* tried to board them. "Sink his boat when it comes alongside," said Breslin. "You have a couple of heavy grindstones. Let us have them ready to heave over the side."

On board the *Catalpa* the atmosphere grew taut with the expectancy of battle. From the *Georgette* nobody on the deck of the *Catalpa* could be seen except Captain Anthony and the lookout man, but the ship was vibrant with activity and tenseness. Crouching under the gunwale, beside the captain, was Breslin, revolver in hand, waiting for the next move. King was lying at a porthole, rifle at the ready. The six rescued men were in the cabin, fully armed, every man resolved to resist until death any attempt at recapture. Desmond and Brennan were at their vantage points, clutching their rifles. If battle was joined, it was to be a fight to the bitter end with no surrender. The first mate, smarting with anger at the insult to the American flag, was in no mood to accommodate any request from the *Georgette*.

The captain reminded him of some short heavy logs in the hold which could be useful as defensive weapons and told him order the crew to bring them on deck. They were quickly passed up and placed on the main hatch, ready for use. The whale lances were got ready as defensive weapons. At this stage there was a diversion. The lookout reported a sail on the lee bow, and looking shoreward they saw a small sail between themselves and Rottnest Island. This drew the captain's attention to his position and, fearing he might be coming too close to land and liable to run into British waters, he wore ship and stood on the other tack, bearing down perilously close on the *Georgette*. The *Georgette* backed hastily out of the way and the party on board looked disconcerted at the move. It looked very like an effort to ram them.

The fifteen minutes' grace, and several more, expired. The *Georgette* steamed slowly across the *Catalpa's* stern and Breslin expected a raking shot amongst the masts. It did not come. The *Georgette* ranged alongside again and it was clear to Breslin that the game of bluff was played out. The men on board the *Georgette* were looking intently through their glasses at every movement on board the *Catalpa*. Their spokesman, whom Breslin thought to be Colonel Harvest, but was in fact Superintendent J. F. Stone, of the water police, called out:

"Won't you surrender to our government?"

To this naive request there was no reply. Again he called out: "I see three of those men on board now."

Captain Anthony replied: "You are mistaken, sir. The men you see are my ship's crew."

The rescued men were all in the cabin from the time the *Georgette* first bore down on the ship, and they had strict orders from Breslin not to come on deck unless he called them. The *Catalpa* held on its course, and the two ships sailed side by side for about ten minutes. Then the *Georgette* hailed again: "Can I come on board?"

Captain Anthony replied: "No, sir; I am bound for sea and can't stop."

This was the last exchange between the two ships. The *Catalpa* sailed on and the *Georgette* still kept her company

There was nothing more Superintendent Stone could do, however. At half-past nine the *Georgette* swung off slowly and steamed back to Fremantle. The *Catalpa* kept steadily on her course, heading south-west. John Breslin and Captain Anthony had won the battle of wits.

We have chiefly been following Breslin's spare but dramatic narrative of these encounters on the high seas. In order to round off the story, it is well to give the Australian version of events which was published very fully in the *Fremantle Herald* and other Western Australian papers. While the substance of both accounts is the same, there are some differences of detail.

According to the Australian version the *Georgette,* on sighting the *Catalpa,* hoisted her pennant and the ensign, and all hands were put under arms. As she did not gain on the *Catalpa* and the wind was freshening, she fired a shot under the whaler's stern. The whaler then ran up the American flag. She took no further notice of the signal, and the *Georgette,* under top steam and all sail, gave full chase. As the *Catalpa* did not attempt to shorten sail, or take any notice of the signal, the *Georgette,* when it had steamed to within a quarter of a mile of her, fired a shot across her bow. The captain of the *Catalpa* then got into the quarter boat. The *Georgette* stood on within hailing distance, and Superintendent J. F. Stone, of the water police, addressed the captain:

"I demand six escaped prisoners now on board this ship, in the name of the government of Western Australia. I know you and your vessel. I know the men I want are on board, for the police saw them go on board yesterday; if you don't give them up you must take the consequences."

The captain answered: "I have no prisoners on board."

Mr. Stone replied: "You have, and I see three of them."

To this the captain replied: "I have no prisoners here, all are seamen belonging to the ship."

The wind was compelling the *Georgette* away from the whaler, and Superintendent Stone now said to the captain: "I will give you fifteen minutes to consider what you will do."

At the end of that time the *Georgette* again went alongside, and Mr. Stone renewed his demand for the prisoners and the captain replied that he had no prisoners on board.

"If you don't give them up," said Mr. Stone, pointing to the gun, "I will fire into you and sink you or disable you."

At this time police and pensioners stood by with arms ready, and there was a man in position at the gun with a lighted match. Nothing alarmed at the threat, the captain coolly replied:

"I don't care what you do. I am on the high seas and that flag protects me." He pointed to the American flag as he spoke.

Mr. Stone replied: "You have escaped convicts on board your ship, a misdemeanour against the laws of this colony, and your flag won't protect you in that."

"Yes it will, or in felony either," replied the captain.

"Will you let me board your ship and see for myself," asked Mr. Stone.

The reply was decisive. "You shan't board my vessel."

"Then your government will be communicated with," said Mr. Stone, "and you must take the consequences."

"All right," said the captain.

That was the end. Mr. Stone had gone as far as he dared, without result, and the *Georgette* returned to Fremantle, which it reached about one o'clock. The crowd which collected at the jetty to hear the outcome of its mission made bets as it approached, some that the *Catalpa* had attacked and beaten her, others that the whaler, overawed by the show of force on the *Georgette*, had quietly surrendered the fugitives. When the facts were made known, some people gave vent to their indignation at the colony having been fooled by a Yankee skipper. The pensioners and police felt they had been taking part in a silly farce, "and had been laughed at by the Yankees at sea, and the public on shore, and sincerely hoped that instructions would be given to go out again and take the prisoners by force." The Governor, however, considered that prudence was the better course. He refused to be led into committing a breach of international law to gratify a feeling of resentment at the "cool effrontery" of the Yankee. He directed that the armed parties be dismissed and the vessel returned to the agent, with his Excellency's thanks to him and to all others who co-operated in the venture. Nor did he forget to express his approbation of Superintendent Stone. In a short time the crew dispersed and, we are told, the town lapsed into its normal condition of quietude, having suffered three days of the most intense excitement ever experienced in its history. Nevertheless, there were some sore hearts amongst the prison authorities.

There was one young man in the crowd who looked on in amused contempt at the incompetence with which the Fremantle authorities handled their side of the affair. He was John Walsh who, along with McCarthy, had cut the telegraph wires and was a witness of all the furore that followed the rescue. He was as hard on his own friends as on the authorities. The rescuers blundered in not having arrested and marooned Bell, but those in charge of the *Georgette* were nothing better than duffers for downright mismanagement. He stated that "if the *Georgette* remained with the *Catalpa* nothing could save them."—(*Devoy's Post Bag* I, page 222). He was quite candid about telling the rescuers, when he got to New York, what he thought of the business. But while on Western Australian territory he kept his thoughts strictly to himself.

Fortune favoured the *Catalpa*. That night the wind rose from the east and later blew into a gale, driving the whaler before it. In 48 hours it was four hundred miles from the Australian coast.

CHAPTER TWENTY-TWO

AUSTRALIAN REACTIONS

THE authorities in Perth now applied themselves to the age-old occupation of locking the stable door after the horse was stolen. It appears that Governor Robinson was more enraged at the prisoners' rescue than one would be led to expect from his suave conduct as reported by the *Fremantle Herald*. A commission was set up to inquire into the prison discipline. The Governor ordered the immediate arrest and return to Fremantle prison under strong police escort of the remaining few Fenians who were on ticket of leave in the colony. Although the records of these men had been exemplary, they were hustled unceremoniously to the prison, a step which a correspondent tells us was "loudly condemned by the press in the colony, and the public was extremely wroth at the injustice perpetrated on these unoffending men."—(*Munster News,* reprinted in *The Irishman,* 15 July 1876). Whatever excuses the Governor might invent, it was clear that he acted in a spirit of reprisal. The same correspondent tells us that the prison authorities were "most unmercifully chaffed" over the escape, and from his description, it is clear that Breslin used his social graces with effect.

It transpired now that "Mr. Collins had so far ingratiated himself with one of the chief officials of the gaol—the clerk of works—that he had him passed through the prison and pointed out, with much exactness, its architectural belongings, and its general security against the escape of its inmates."

The colony's detective force shared the blame for being so obtuse as not to have suspected Mr. Collins's true purpose in the colony, and for having learned nothing of his pursuits during the four or five months he had stayed in the Emerald Isle Hotel as a gentleman of private means. Patrick Maloney, the proprietor of the hotel, came in for his share of official attention because, being an Irishman and friendly as a matter of course with all the Fenians at large, it was strongly suspected that he had been aware all along of Mr. Collins's mission. He was interviewed by the detectives, "but Mr. Patrick Maloney, County Clare, had not been for some years in the constabulary at Ennis and afterwards at Limerick, without having acquired enough of that rare adroitness earned by commerce with such service, to be a match for any policeman in the antipodes." So the detectives did not get much change out of him, nor could they discover that he had had any complicity in the affair, or that he knew more about Collins than the general public, which put the enigmatic visitor down variously as an intending squatter, sheep farmer or mining speculator on a large scale after the fashion of Yankees.

Corroboration of the vindictive behaviour of the Perth authorities is found in a letter from Western Australia to a resident of Virginia city, Nevada, published in part in the New York *Irish World* of 19 August 1876. The Australian letter says:

> You cannot imagine the excitement caused by this escape . . . It seems that the Governor was extremely annoyed . . . One thing this escape has been the cause of which I regret—those unfortunate men who were out of prison by what is called "ticket of leave" had their tickets revoked, and those others who were employed about the town in gangs are now kept within the prison wall in close confinement. I do not know if this be the work of the Governor or of his subordinates, but, truly, whoever had the doing of it has no need to be proud of it, for it is an act worthy of a slave driver. The big-wigs held, for a week or more, an enquiry, and I understand that they tried hard to bring some of the unfortunate subordinate officers into a scrape; however, I understand that the plan did not succeed and everyone has been acquitted of blame in the matter. The public appear to be in favour of the escapes, and even the worst enemy amongst us does not wish for the capture of the prisoners, but merely for the sending back of the "notorious Collins," the supposed leader of the expedition. Opinions even as regards him are divided, some being for hanging, and others—amongst them the ladies—for letting him escape.

The "unfortunate men" referred to were soldier Fenians, most of whom had short sentences. There were six of them, and three of them had actually completed their terms, but this did not save them from official revenge. In the general round up of suspects, John Walsh and Denis Florence McCarthy, who had aided the escape effectively by cutting the telegraph wires, were arrested. They were held for some time, but nothing could be proved against them, so they were released. They later left for the eastern colonies and went from there to America. McCarthy was still living in Chicago in 1904. Walsh, after an eventful career, died in poverty in New York in the '80's.

Naturally the Tory press of Western Australia flashed forth in anger. "It seems humiliating," said the *Perth Enquirer*, "that a Yankee, with half a dozen coloured men, should be able to come into our waters and carry off six of the most determined of the Fenian convicts—all the unreleased of the military prisoners—and then to laugh at us for allowing them to be taken away without securing them." *The Enquirer* adds a detail to our knowledge of the affair which proves that precautions were taken by the rescuers in a most thoroughgoing manner. "It would appear," it states, "that there was a desire to obtain correct legal information on international law, for about the time of Captain Anthony's visit to Fremantle, Johnson [i.e. Tom Desmond] called upon Mr. Howell, the solicitor in Perth, and asked him several questions as to the limit of neutral waters, from which we would infer that the Captain knew what he was about when he told Mr. Stone that his flag protected him where he then was against misdemeanour or felony either."—(*Perth Enquirer*, 26 April, reprinted in *The Irishman*, 15 July 1876).

The Enquirer hoped that her Majesty's ships would give full chase to the whaler and bring the fugitives back to their cells, "but," it adds on a final note of pessimism, "we fear not."

At the other end of Australia the *Melbourne Argus* described the event in Fremantle as a grave international outrage. It was precisely as if a French boat were to run across to Portland and take away from there all the convicts she had room for. The Imperial authorities were bound to take notice of this outrage and to demand substantial redress. The offence was too glaring to be overlooked and the *Argus* presumed that "important communications" would speedily pass between the governments of Westminster and Washington. Wisely enough, it made no attempt to forecast what their outcome might be.

The *Melbourne Advocate*, on the other hand, retained a calm detachment about the whole affair and did not withhold its admiration for the skill and daring with which the rescue was carried out.

And done so easily that one's surprise is much heightened by that fact. If the six Fenians were freemen, and all the inhabitants of Fremantle were buried in profound sleep, the affair could not have been managed more quietly. The feeling of irritation at this whole business is very strong in Fremantle and naturally so, for it is no trifle that men who were rebels while they wore the uniform of the Queen, and whom her Majesty's ministers refused over and over again to recommend to her clemency, have taken French leave of their jailers; and it is still more irritating that an accomplice in their flight, standing under the United States flag, and relying on it as a protecting aegis, defied an English vessel, legally commissioned, to capture the fugitives by force.—(*Melbourne Advocate,* reprinted in the Liverpool *United Irishman,* 5 August 1876).

The *Advocate* readily agreed with the *Perth Inquirer* that it *was* humiliating and it likewise had pleasure in agreeing with its local contemporary, the *Argus,* when the latter presumed that the "important communications" would be opened up at once between London and Washington. That, stated the *Advocate,* was exactly what would occur. But there would be no dénouement. The correspondence would be voluminous and long drawn out but very courteous on both sides, for why should first cousins presiding over the destinies of the English-speaking world quarrel over half a dozen unfortunate Irishmen? Westminster was not without a case against Washington over this Fenian business, but then the converse was just as true, so that, when all was said and done, the argument would taper down "to an indivisible (and invisible) point." In other words it would end in smoke.

"It is to be regretted," the *Advocate* went on, "that the direct ocean cable is not now working so that the Imperial government might be apprised without delay of the escape of the Fenians, and Westminster could immediately commence the important correspondence between the two governments."

One might wonder whether the writings of the *Melbourne Advocate* were the work of a fine Hibernian hand or were inspired by some recondite Irish-republican influence, because the editor was obviously laughing up his sleeve.

In point of fact, the direct ocean cable was not working. An I.R.B. detachment had seen to that. It was cut on 27 April between Australia and Java, evidently by previous arrangement, both as a signal to America that the rescue was successful and, as the *Times* correspondent put it, "to prevent news being sent out which might facilitate British war vessels in making pursuit."—(*The Irishman,* 1 July 1876). That it was the work of Irish republicans is evident from a letter of Dr. William Carroll of Philadelphia to John Devoy dated 29 April 1876, which says:

> Yours of yesterday is just to hand. I hope your surmise as to the cause of "the cable" being "broken" is correct. If so, and all goes well with our friends, it will electrify our people the world over.—(*Devoy's Post Bag,* I, 167).

From this it will be seen that Devoy and Carroll had been apprised of the rescue in little over a week from the time it was carried out. This was quick work.

CHAPTER TWENTY-THREE

A DEBATE AND AN ENLIGHTENMENT

WITH the exception of Devoy and his committee, the northern hemisphere had as yet no intimation of the rescue when the debate opened in the House of Commons on Monday 22 May on the subject of an amnesty for the Fenian prisoners still held in English jails. Besides those who were supposed to be jailed in Western Australia there was also a small group of Fenians behind bars in England. Michael Davitt was the most notable of these, but the number included Edward O'Meagher Condon and Patrick Meledy, two men serving sentence for taking part in the rescue at Manchester in 1867 during which Sergeant Brett had been accidentally killed, and Davitt's colleague John Wilson, an Englishman who, though not a Fenian himself, proved faithful to the Fenian cause by remaining silent about what he knew of its secrets.

The occasion chosen for a plea for clemency was opportune. Queen Victoria had assumed the new title of Empress of India. The Prince of Wales had just concluded a brilliant and successful tour throughout the dominions. A petition for clemency was presented to Parliament, signed by 138 members of the House of Commons, including such prominent names as Jacob Bright, A. J. Mundella, Samuel Plimsoll and Charles Dilke. The Liverpool *United Irishman*, which was the organ of the Home Rule Confederation of Great Britain, tells us (27 May 1876) that the amount of interest which this question had awakened and the anxiety with which Mr. Disraeli's reply was looked forward to had been evoked on very few public occasions. Mr. M. Brooks, M.P., Lord Mayor of Dublin, introduced the topic by asking the First Lord of the Treasury if it was his intention to advise her Majesty to extend her royal mercy to the prisoners still suffering punishment for offences in breach of their allegiance to her Majesty.

Mr. Disraeli replied. He considered the cases of Davitt, Wilson, O'Meagher Condon and Meledy in words which showed that they could expect no sympathy and dismissed at once the plea for clemency on their behalf. He went on:

All the rest of the military convicts have been transported to Western Australia; and with regard to them, before I answered the Question of the hon. Gentleman I should have made myself acquainted with their exact and precise position. It is from no want of pains on my part that I have not succeeded in obtaining that information, for I should like to know the exact condition of those persons. Two ot them have, I understand, worked out their time, and are now free, and I cannot but believe, from something that has reached me at different times in regard to this matter, that those who are not free are in a position very different from that which is generally contemplated in this House as being connected with the condition of convicts in a state of penal servitude; and I would remind hon. Gentlemen that if pardons were offered to any individuals who had connected themselves with those disturbances in Ireland it is not highly improbable that conditions would be insisted on in those pardons by which those receiving them would be compelled to absent themselves from this country. [Hear, hear!]. That assent only proves that it may not be impossible that many of those convicts in Western Australia are, in fact, at this moment, enjoying a state of existence that their friends in this House are quite prepared they should accept . . . I am bound to say that I am not prepared to advise her Majesty to release the prisoners referred to in the question of the hon. Gentleman.—(*Hansard,* Vol. CCXXIX, Cols. 1040-52. Debate of 22 May 1876).

There was sharp disappointment in Irish circles over the Prime Minister's reply, as well for its manner as for its matter. The Liverpool *United Irishman* called it "a plain, unvarnished and heartless" answer. An Irish witness of the scene in the Commons, Frank Hugh O'Donnell, M.P., states that Disraeli was in "his most imperial and superior mood" on the occasion, that his manner "suggested base, low instincts and tendencies in the Fenians, even more than his phrases" and that "if he had deliberately desired to work mischief in Ireland and throughout the Irish race, he could not have done better." (F. H. O'Donnell, *History of the Irish Parliamentary Party,* I, 157).

The fiery and flamboyant correspondent of the New York *Irish World,* Thomas Mooney (Transatlantic), also present, states that

the expression of his whole person, face, mouth and eyes, at the supreme moment when he sat down declaring against the prisoners' release, was one of royal contempt towards the Irish nation, its martyrs and its advocates.—(*Irish World,* 24 June 1876).

In the debate which followed, Joe Biggar rubbed it in by stating (amid cries of Oh! Oh!):

It is generally supposed that the commander-in-chief of the forces is one of those who has great objection to the remission of these sentences. That is not strange in a country which has intrusted the command of the army to a German prince not identified with England.—(Liverpool *United Irishman,* 27 May 1876).

Amongst those who spoke in favour of amnesty was one C. S. Parnell.

That part of Disraeli's speech dealing with the "exact condition" of the Western Australian prisoners, and their "enjoying a state of existence which their friends in this House are quite prepared they should accept" had a touch of unintended humour which was heartily enjoyed by its Irish readers when the facts became known. It was suggested in

John Denvir's *United Irishman,* 10 June, that Disraeli must have known of the escape and the failure of recapture on the night of the debate, and that his ambiguous language, in the light of later knowledge, pointed to the conclusion. This is very unlikely as the writer assumed that the telegraph route from Australia, by which the news would swiftly reach London, was open all along, which it was not. In any case, the rescue had rendered the House of Commons debate to a great extent nugatory.

London first heard of it on 6 June by despatch from Melbourne. About the same time the S.S. *Colima* from Sydney reached San Francisco with similar news and the information that the Australia-Java cable was broken on 27 April. When the tidings became known throughout North America and Europe the exultation of the Irish race knew no bounds. O'Donovan Rossa saw the people dancing with joy in the streets of Omaha. John Boyle O'Reilly wrote to Devoy on 10 June that, as soon as the news became known, the Boston papers stormed his office for interviews. They knew he had been a prisoner in Australia and thought he had something to do with it. O'Reilly was cautious in giving them information at this early stage, and withheld the names of the captain and ship. The *Times* correspondent told his paper that the name of the ship was a closely guarded secret. Yet somehow or other the New Bedford papers found out and published the names of both. One Boston paper copied the names, but O'Reilly got the others to omit them. The general impression was that the *Catalpa* was coming to San Francisco and this notion was probably encouraged by Devoy and his colleagues in order to divert attention from Fernandina, Florida, where they had arranged that it should arrive.

Popular reaction to the news in America is indicated by the opinions of leading papers which could in no way be described as under Irish influence. The *New York Tribune* stated:

Few will deny the Irish prisoners who have escaped from Australia the right to freedom.—(Reprinted in *The Irishman,* 1 July 1876).

The *New York World* wrote:

The news of the escape . . . with the friendly help of an American whaler, will be very generally received, even in England, we suspect, without much regret. In this country everybody will be cordially pleased.—*(ibid.)*.

The views of the *New York Herald*, which was controlled by James Gordon Bennett, and had a large Irish staff, might have been prompted by Devoy, who was night editor. It said:

This carefully prepared plan to rescue a number of sentenced prisoners, insignificant, perhaps, in themselves, shows they were estimated by their brethren for their sacrifices as much as for their personal value, and the demonstration of this alone will, doubtless, stimulate the anti-English sentiment among the mass of Irishmen opposed to English rule. The affair will bring little credit to Mr. Disraeli, who so recently refused to remit the penalties of these men.—*(ibid.)*.

Similarly the influential *Philadelphia Times* might have been echoing the views of Dr. William Carroll, who was a close friend of editor McClure, when it said that "enthusiasm was unbounded" and hinted that the event would act as a stimulus to O'Donovan Rossa's Skirmishing Fund, recently opened for warlike operations against England. The Irish-American papers gave expression to the wild exultation of Irish nationalists at the success of the *Catalpa* expedition, but the Boston *Pilot*, in particular, struck a very significant note when it said that a valuable lesson from the rescue had a bearing on the English army. The thousands of Irishmen in the ranks of the British army knew that these men were kept in prison *because they had been soldiers*. No one seemed to care for them.

To see their comrades forgotten and left to rot in their dungeons was enough to make the Irishmen of the army abjure their nationality and accept the English dominion in Ireland.

This has been averted by the rescue. The soldiers in the English army will read the news with a deeper thrill than any other Irishmen. It has a larger meaning to them than to other. "Now," they will say, "now, at last, we are a part of the Irish people. Our red coats do not separate us from our countrymen; and if we suffer for their cause, they will be true as steel to us in the day of trial."—(*The Pilot*, 24 June 1876, reprinted in *The Catalpa Expedition*, 204-5).

The writer of this was the one-time officer of the Tenth Hussars, John Boyle O'Reilly. In Dublin the escape was celebrated by a great demonstration. With 500 torchbearers leading, a vast concourse marched from St. Catherine's Church, Thomas Street (where Robert Emmet was executed) through the Cornmarket, High Street, Cork Hill, College Green and Westmoreland Street to Nelson's Pillar, where it turned into Henry Street and marched by way of Mary Street and Capel Street to Grattan Bridge. Here the procession halted and, amidst cheers, two effigies, one of Prime Minister Disraeli and the other of the Duke of Cambridge, both decorated with uncomplimentary placards, were hoisted over the parapet and burned. The leading Tory paper of Dublin, the *Daily Express,* was very angry. It protested against any repeat of this "Saturnalia" and paid no compliment to the administration of Western Australia by saying it was unfortunate that "through the negligence or connivance of colonial officials, the prisoners have been allowed to escape." It was perfectly shocking that the quiet of the streets on a Sunday evening should be disturbed by the discordant sounds of Fenian music, the singing of Fenian songs, and insults to the Prime Minister. "All these are elements of social mischief," warned the choleric *Express. Saunders Newsletter,* not a nationalist organ, described the demonstration as an orderly one, organised by the Dublin working classes, with "not an intoxicated individual to be seen." (Reports reprinted in *The Irishman,* 17 June 1876). In a paean of exultation the leading article in *The Irishman* of 10 June gave expression to the common feelings of Irishmen:

> Easter Monday was the day of days for them. They had heard the glad Alleluiah in the chapels, telling that Death had been conquered, and the Grave made to give up its dead. They were dead—was there to be a call to life sped to them, even there in the dark Sepulchre of Slavery, amid the corruption of sin and crime? . . . They pass from Fetters to Freedom.

There was some high and holy Tory anger in London. Although the *Annual Register* for 1876 is shy to the point of silence, the press was not quite so inarticulate. The *Daily*

Telegraph declared that the skipper of the *Catalpa,* like most Yankee mariners an accomplished sea-lawyer, sailed off in triumph, laughing at the scrupulous British deference to international law. "This is a humiliating result." If the American vessel took the convicts on board in Australian, that is British waters, then the *Telegraph* presumed that Britain could "insist on their rendition and on redress in some shape for a violation of our sovereignty." The government might be excused for being "firm and peremptory" in calling attention to this violation of law by the Yankee whaler. The American correspondent of *The Times* was perturbed. It was of course, he conceded, a great triumph for the Fenians but fraught with peril to the friendly relations between Britain and America.

> When the whaler comes into an American port and lands her passengers, the British authorities, it seems, might have very good ground for interference, and it is difficult to see how the United States could avoid giving up the prisoners and punishing the vessel and, if they can be found, those engaged in the rescue.—(*The Irishman,* 1 July 1876).

The Times correspondent could hardly have been less realistic in his appreciation of America's opinion. There was not the remotest possibility of any such turn of events. This was more or less recognised in the attitude taken by *The Times* itself. It was deplorable, but true, that Irishmen would take an almost sadistic delight in managing affairs in such a way as to disconcert this great newspaper. On the rescue of the Australian prisoners it offered the following observations:

> The story which comes to us from west Australia of the escape of the Fenian prisoners from the convict settlement at Fremantle is in many ways remarkable. It is not, however, as some Americans seem to think, a humiliating story for this country. It is quite true that the government of this country, though it could not assent to such arguments as those by which Mr. Bright the other day endeavoured to justify the conditional release of convicted murderers or military traitors, is not sorry to be rid, by whatever means, of a barren and burdensome responsibility. But to relieve the British government from a difficulty assuredly did not enter the motives of the American

conspirators, who planned and carried out the rescue at Fremantle. We have to look at that act strictly from the point of view of international duty, and without reference to the further question how far it may be worth while to demand explanations of an audacious outrage. Regarded in itself, the conduct of the rescuers was wholly without legal justification or palliation; if not in the correct sense of the term piratical, it was, at any rate, a bad example of filibustering; and that any Americans who have a sense of national self-respect should exult in the success of such a paltry trick for evasion of justice is beyond an Englishman's comprehension. Nothing could be more prosaic, and indeed, mean, than the details of the plot which was successful in releasing six of the Fenian prisoners held in custody in west Australia . . . For security against such lawless evasions we have to trust chiefly to the comity of nations, and the reciprocity that is enforced upon civilised communities by a sense of common needs. The American government and the American people are bound to ask themselves whether it is tolerable that such piratical enterprises directed against the public justice of a friendly state should be allowed to go unpunished. Though mobs and newspapers in the United States often talk mischievous nonsense, the American government is generally sober and sagacious in its practical policy, and we cannot believe that it will fail to mark its severe disapproval of a filibustering expedition on friendly soil like that planned in New York and accomplished in west Australia. In the meantime, the temper of suspicion which such outrages naturally induce may aggravate the hardships of a convict's life. At present detention in this remote place of exile has been compatible with considerable liberty of movement. It may be worth while suggesting to the zealous friends of men whom we hold to be felons and they hold to be patriots, that, if such enterprises as this at Fremantle are indulged in, those charged with the safekeeping of the convicts may, very reluctantly, for their own protection, be forced to curtail the privileges these men now enjoy.—(*The Times,* 7 August 1876).

This was neither well nor wisely said. A retort was not long in coming from the New York daily, *The World,* which spoke with authority, not for the Irish race specifically, but for the extensive body of American opinion which was unfriendly towards England. *The World* set out in detail what might be called the popular American view of the incident, coloured to some extent, no doubt, by hostile memories of Britain's attitude during the late Civil War, but held with strong conviction, and received with huge approbation by Irishmen:

The complaint of the London *Times* in regard to the assistance rendered by Americans in the escape of the Fenian prisoners from west Australia was not conceived in good taste, and has been brought forth in very bad temper.

England has always been a place of refuge—a true "Alsatia"—for political offenders against other countries, and Englishmen are so jealous of the right of asylum that they protect known forgers or defaulters rather than carry out the provisions of a treaty which might possibly in the remote future be construed so as to bring about the surrender of a political prisoner. London has been for years the home of refugees from continental Europe. Rather than surrender her right to protect political rebels, England in 1853 risked a war with France on behalf of Bernard, the accomplice of Orsini, in an atrocious assassination. Mazzini, Struve, Prim, and hosts of others have planned in England, some of them murder, and others revolution, in perfect security. English volunteers never hesitated out of reverence to "the public justice of a friendly State," to take a hand in aid of Garibaldi or of Jefferson Davis or of any other man, patriot or conspirator, who happened to be striking against the existing order of things in his own country . . . It is rather cool of England, then, to be annoyed when other nations adopt her own opinions in regard to baffled revolutionists and political prisoners generally . . . We venture to say that no vessel flying the British flag would refuse upon the high seas to receive fugitives escaping from the political prisons of any other nation. Technically, the American ship which rescued the Fenians has done no more than this, *and all talk about demanding redress is mere nonsense.*

The *Catalpa* may have gone to the Australian coast with the design of rescuing the Fenian prisoners, but she kept on the high seas, and in no way compromised her flag. The men who planned the escape, and effected it at their own proper risk, were doubtless Irishmen—partakers, it may be, in the conspiracy for which the prisoners were suffering. In their eyes the convicts were not criminals but martyrs.

. . . They owed neither courtesy nor comity to the British government, at the hands of which the greatest favour they had to expect would be a commutation of the death-penalty into penal servitude for life. They did owe something to the comrades whom they had perhaps originally helped to lead into danger, and they quitted themselves of their obligation like good men and true. The only part, so far as yet appears, which any American took in the affair, was one which eminently befits an American, that of receiving under the Stars and Stripes fugitives whose greatest crime was their uncalculating and foolhardy zeal for their native land.

Nations which find it necessary to fill penal colonies with political convicts must not insist upon the sympathy and help of other countries in the task of guarding them. If it was a legitimate employment of English capital for English shipowners to make a regular trade of running the blockade with supplies to the confederates during our Civil War, it certainly is fair enough for New Bedford whalers, if they are paid for the business, to stand off and on twenty or thirty miles from the coast of west Australia and pick up political prisoners, who may swim or row out to them, as John Boyle O'Reilly did formerly, and as Wilson and his companions have now done . . .

It is safe to say that if that Journal [*The Times*] wants to make Fenian prisoners more anxious to escape and their countrymen in all parts of the world more eager to aid them and Americans more heartily satisfied to see their efforts crowned with success, it cannot do better than keep on advocating that the remaining convicts shall be submitted to unusual restraints and annoyances by way of vengeance for the escape of their fellows.—(Reprinted in *The Irishman,* 23 September 1876).

To this *The Times* made no reply. As for the "voluminous correspondence" which the Melbourne papers surmised would pass between Washington and Westminster, no word of it has ever been made public, that is if it exists at all. Nor does history record whether the Duke of Cambridge had anything to say about the matter.

CHAPTER TWENTY-FOUR

HOMEWARD BOUND

THE *Catalpa* sailed across the Indian Ocean, passing by the south end of Madagascar, now the Malagasi Republic, rounded the Cape of Good Hope, avoided St. Helena and Ascension Isle in its northward course and crossed the Equator at long. 31°W. on 10 July. It would be pleasant to relate that the voyage back, even if the seas were not always smooth, was marked by cordial relations between all, and that the rescued men showed a proper appreciation of the debt of gratitude which they owed to their rescuers.

Human nature, however, does not conform to an ideal. Otherwise this story would read like a fairytale. Great courage and extreme pettiness can exist side by side in the same person, a fact which in no way reduces their stature as men. What we are relating is a true story about real people and their reactions to each other and to their environment.

The long years of imprisonment and strain had told heavily on the fibre of the Fenian soldiers. In the confined quarters of the whaler, tempers were liable to become frayed and grievances, whether real or fancied, to increase out of proportion.

But the absolute menace to good relations was Thomas Brennan. From the time that Captain Anthony had declined to take him ashore at St. Michael's in the Azores, a disgruntled, carping, mischievous spirit had rankled in his mind against Breslin, Devoy and the other chief promoters of the enterprise, John W. Goff excepted. He was, of course, Goff's special protégé. He found an ally in Denis Duggan, who had been taken on as ship's carpenter. Duggan felt resentful towards Breslin because he had been kept on board ship all the time in Western Australia and had been allotted no place in the scheme of rescue. The place which would have been his was given to John King, whom Breslin preferred for the part, owing to his Australian experience.

Breslin's report of the return voyage, which he submitted to the Clan na Gael points the finger of blame directly at these two men. "We had not been at sea a fortnight," states Breslin, "when I was informed by one of the prisoners that Brennan meant to do me all the mischief he could, and I shortly after learned that Duggan and he combined for that purpose."

It appears that Brennan gave the ex-prisoners to understand he was a man of great importance in the Clan na Gael organisation and that Breslin was a kind of interloper who had only lately joined. Duggan confirmed this impression to the prisoners and told the mate that Brennan had more authority in the plan of rescue than Breslin. Duggan also told the men that provisions specially shipped for their use, such as canned meats, fruit and condensed milk, had been given to the crew and to other ships. It was understood that Brennan was taking notes of all these alleged shortcomings and deficiencies and threatening to have Captain Anthony denounced. Brennan added to the men's discontent by saying that the organisation was strong in money and ought to have provided "delicacies" for them, meaning whiskey. John Devoy considered that if the men had stayed "dry" for ten years they could easily stay so for another four months. If any quantity of whiskey had been put aboard it would have aroused immediate suspicion. Besides, Captain Anthony would not have it. He was a strict teetotaller and carried only a small quantity of New England rum and brandy in the medicine cabinet.

On the surface, things ran smoothly enough, but underneath discontent was rife. Breslin reported with stinging sarcasm that things came to such a pass that, in his belief, the men considered themselves injured by having been taken on board the *Catalpa*. Harrington said they were better treated on board the convict ship, for they got a glass of wine every day. Cranston wished himself back in Fremantle one morning that the flapjacks were not fried as he liked them; Hogan suffered agonies because the cook would not supply him with boiled onions; Hassett complained that he was deprived of his liberty on board the *Catalpa*. Wilson complained he could not eat the food, said he was weakening every day and would die if not put ashore soon. Darragh was the only one of the six for whom Breslin could say a good word. One might think Breslin was severe in his verdict, but his opinion is sustained, at any rate, by what happened on 27 July.

The *Catalpa* was at that time in latitude 20° 12″ N. and longitude 46°W. At one p.m. they sighted a ship steering west, flying the American colours. It was the first American ship they had met since leaving Australia. Captain Anthony said he would go on board to see if he could buy any sugar or molasses, because the *Catalpa's* supply had run out, and to get any news he could. When Captain Anthony had shoved off in the boat, Wilson came up to Breslin and said he wanted to be put ashore if that ship was going to an American port. Breslin pointed out to him that the ship was probably bound for Barbados for sugar, and he could not say whether Captain Anthony could get aboard her or not, as it was the first mate's opinion his boat could not overtake her.

Wilson charged him bluntly. "You refuse to put me on board. Life is life. My health is getting worse every day. I want to be put on shore."

Breslin pointed out that he had not refused to send him on shore, but had only explained the situation to him. "But," he added, "you can note down, if you like, that I have refused. Life is life to me as much as to you, and I believe we are all anxious to get on shore."

Wilson was in an ugly mood, and his manner was insolent as he replied: "We ought all to be on shore long ago, and might have been only for you."

Words like these were bound to create trouble. Captain Anthony's errand turned out to be fruitless. The passing ship was the *Kentuckian* of Boston, from Liverpool bound for New Orleans. She had hardly enough provisions for her own crew and was in such haste that Captain Anthony remained only a few minutes on board and came away with just a few newspapers. So Wilson's hopes of being taken ashore on that ship were dashed. Mischief, however, was afoot. The intention of the promoters of the expedition had been that the *Catalpa*, having carried out the rescue, should cruise for whale on the return journey. In this way it was hoped to earn the money which must be refunded to those Clan na Gael clubs which had loaned money out of the revolutionary fund. Then, when a profitable amount of whaling had been done, the rescued men were to be landed at Fernandina, Florida, where the port collector, a friend of Senator Conover's, would receive them and arrange for their further journey to New York.

This intention could not be carried out because the prisoners refused to co-operate in it. On the afternoon of the day they met the *Kentuckian*, Duggan, Brennan and Desmond requested a private talk with Breslin, Captain Anthony withdrew from the cabin and Breslin asked the men to be seated. Brennan opened the conversation. He stated that as members of the organisation they found fault with Breslin's conduct on board ship, that he directed the movements of the ship without consulting them, which was wrong, that the rescued men were suffering from ill-health, that the food was unsuited to them and that they should be put ashore at Fernandina or some other port without delay. Brennan stated in addition that the men believed they would not be free until they landed on American soil. He himself and Duggan believed it would give greater satisfaction to the organisation to put into port at once than to remain out four weeks longer and chance the taking of fourteen thousand dollars worth of oil. Finally, they requested that Breslin should ask Captain Anthony to take them into port.

Breslin asked if that was all, to which they replied that it was. The first part of the charge Breslin answered by asking Brennan to point out a single instance in which he had taken charge of the ship or conducted himself otherwise than as a passenger since the *Catalpa* left the shores of Western Australia, apart from the morning they first boarded her on escaping, on which occasion he required nothing from them but to obey orders. Brennan hedged and had to admit that he could point to no instance whatever. Breslin then said, regarding the food, that he had been used himself to as good food as any man on board, and that every man on the ship was given the same as was served to himself. They would all have been very glad to get on board at Fremantle with the prospect of much harder fare. Every one of the rescued men had improved in appearance since coming on board, and the two men who were complaining of ill-health had suffered in the same manner for years, so that their complaints could in no way be put down to the voyage. In fact, the voyage appeared to benefit them more than otherwise.

Brennan agreed that all the men had improved in appearance. Duggan was convinced that they had not. Breslin said he was perfectly satisfied with the captain's conduct, and that he was acting in the best interests of the owners in wanting to prolong the cruise a little for oil, and that he, Breslin, knew of no better chance to make the same amount of money for the organisation in the same time. Brennan and Duggan stated that there was money enough in the organisation, and that it would give greater satisfaction to have the men home for the forthcoming Clan na Gael convention. Breslin pointed out, in regard to the men's fears for their freedom, that this question had been decided off Fremantle; when the British did not dare to take them almost in their own waters on that occasion, they would never attempt to interfere with them on the shores of America. He believed the American flag protected them as much now as then, and the men were as free as if they were on American soil. Duggan agreed with this, but said the prisoners could not be got to believe it. Breslin told the men that he did not see sufficient grounds for interfering with the captain and would not do so. Duggan then said that if Paddy Lennon or Michael Cody were in his place either of them would have no hesitation in taking the ship from the captain. Breslin asked him if he thought the Clan na Gael organisation would back them up in such a case. Duggan wasn't too sure.

It was a long and angry discussion. In the course of it Brennan said he had been sent out to watch the interests of the organisation, and that he had been watching its interests for six years. In the course of a controversy which arose later in connection with the expedition, John W. Goff stated that it was necessary to have one honest man aboard, meaning Brennan, on which Devoy sarcastically commented that no doubt it was, in order to keep John Devoy from running away with ship, crew, prisoners and all. It became clear, too, in the course of this discussion that the anxiety of Duggan and Brennan to be home in time for the annual Clan convention had as much to do with the matter as the alleged ill-health of the prisoners. Tom Desmond proposed that they should write out a protest against the ship being stopped on the whaling grounds as Captain Anthony intended. Breslin agreed that if they took the responsibility of guaranteeing Captain Anthony that, by going into port, he would be giving the greater satisfaction to his owners, he, Breslin, would act on it. That evening Breslin received the following note:

On Board Bark *Catalpa*,
July 27th, 1876.

John Breslin:

We the undersigned do hereby request that this ship be brought into port without delay for the following reasons:

1st. Owing to the innutricious quality of the food, the ex-prisoners believe it injurious to their health.

2nd. Owing to the ill-health of some of the ex-prisoners it is deemed dangerous to prolong the voyage.

3rd. The ex-prisoners consider themselves not actually free men until placed on American soil.

4th. By complying with the above we believe it will be satisfactory to all parties interested in this undertaking.

Thos. Desmond, Thomas Brennan, Denis Duggan, John King, Martin J. Hogan, James Wilson, Robert Cranston, Thomas H. Hassett, M. Harrington, T. Darragh.

Breslin called together the men who had signed the note and asked them if they were clear about the nature of the request they had made. He read the note back to them, paragraph by paragraph, and refused to endorse the opinions in the first and second paragraphs, giving his reasons. He then pointed out to the men that compliance with their request would compel Captain Anthony to throw away an almost certain chance of making from ten to fifteen thousand dollars for the organisation. This made no impression. They said they understood the meaning of their request and would rather the ship brought them directly into port. Still Breslin fought for the chance to have the instructions of the Clan fully carried out. From the time they had left the Australian shore, he said, not a minute had been lost in making the swiftest progress they could towards home. If there had been bad weather, he argued, they might have been held back much longer than a month despite all efforts to make a port; the whaling grounds were within six or seven days' sail and only there would any delay become likely. Duggan agreed that no time had been lost in making the voyage, but they all stuck to their demand that the ship should make port at once.

Breslin then laid their protest before the captain and explained to him the state of feeling among the men. He told the captain he had found out that a man, whose signature was attached to the protest, had claimed to have more authority from the owners of the vessel, more influence with them and a greater interest in their concerns than he, Breslin, had himself. Captain Anthony said that Duggan had already intimated as much to him. Breslin told the captain he believed that this impression had been made very strongly on the minds of the ex-prisoners, also that the belief had been instilled in them that they were being treated shabbily and in a manner much different from what their friends had provided for them. After consultation, the captain and Breslin drafted the following reply, which was returned to the signers of the protest:

Gentlemen:

In reply to your note read this evening I beg to state:

The food on board the *Catalpa* is good, sound, ordinary ship's food; the water is good and in sufficient quantity.

The ex-prisoners are in as good a state of health to-day as when they came on board.

The ex-prisoners are anxious to get on shore, believing they are not free men until placed on American soil.

The ex-prisoners take the responsibility of all loss to the owners incurred by my compliance with their request to go into port.

The signers take equal responsibility with the ex-prisoners.

We endorse this statement as correct, and request the captain to go into port.

Denis Duggan, Thos. Desmond, Thos. Brennan, John King, Martin J. Hogan, Thomas H. Hassett, James Wilson, M. Harrington, Robert Cranston, Thomas Darragh.

Breslin read this reply to the men who had put their names to the protest. After a brief discussion they all signed it. Breslin then told Captain Anthony that, under the circumstances, and considering the discontent and ill-feeling amongst the men, he felt justified in taking the ship into port, and asked him to steer for New York. At the time they were steering north by west. It had been their intention to pass through western whaling grounds. There they would be in the track of homeward bound American vessels, and would have a chance of meeting an American vessel willing to take the ex-prisoners on shore. This would leave the *Catalpa* free to cruise the season out. Else they could get all the fresh provisions they needed from some of the whalers cruising there and remain out a month extra in pursuit of whales. This they could have done without any danger or inconvenience. The attitude of the rescued men had altered all that part of the plan. Course was set for New York, it being now too late to put in at Fernandina. For other reasons as well, Breslin had decided not to go there.

After breakfast the following morning Breslin told the men that the ship was going into port. He asked them to take notice that they had forced the captain to do this contrary to the best interests of the vessel's owners, and before any delay had occurred, or any chance to put them ashore had been neglected.

The behaviour of Brennan and Duggan had thoroughly disgusted Breslin. In his full report to the Clan na Gael organisation, dated 17 April 1877, to which he put his name after swearing "to the matter herein contained that came under his own personal observation," he deals in strongly accusatory language with these two men.

He said they were the chief cause of the discontent and ill-feeling. He understood, when leaving New York for Australia, that they could be relied on to help him in every way. He received no assistance from them in any way, but on the contrary both of them had misrepresented every act of his to the men and stated their determination to get him into trouble when they got home, and they had done this while presenting an outward appearance of friendship and agreement with everything he had done. Duggan had stated he would not stay out two days longer even if, by so doing, it meant catching ten thousand dollars worth of oil. Of all the men, Darragh alone proved himself reasonable, and was willing to stay out longer so as to catch whales.

Breslin considered that all the ex-prisoners had improved in health. Wilson and Harrington had chronic ailments, and it was these two men who complained most frequently of ill-health. Wilson used get a pain in the chest which he thought was heart disease. The pain was always relieved by a stimulant called "pain killer" or by a glass of rum or brandy, and he told Breslin the pains were less frequent on board ship than they had been in Fremantle.

Harrington, whose ailment was dysentery, was given a bottle of patent medicine by the mate which made him, according to his own account, better than he had been for years. The two men had been working daily at the harbour construction works in Fremantle as able-bodied men, under the observation of competent medical officers. Breslin was no easy man to fool. He had four years' hospital experience and claimed to know the symptoms of ill-health. There was nothing in the appearance of these two men which indicated an increase of it to him. Yet Breslin, harsh as his judgment may be, pays tribute, rather drily, to the men where he considers it deserved. "Of the general conduct of the men I have no reason to complain," he stated. "On the contrary, it has been rather better than I expected to find it." Anyone taking the ex-prisoners' point of view might be excused for pointing to John Boyle O'Reilly's judgment of Breslin as "somewhat cynical, perhaps, and often stubbornly prejudiced and unjust," only he must be reminded that O'Reilly described him at the same time as a man of few words, of small acquaintance, of culture and refinement behind a modest exterior, in thought and appearance eminently a gentleman, in demeanour dignified and reserved, in observance rather distrustful as if disappointed in his ideal man, a lover of literature, an extraordinary personality hidden behind a barrier of reserve.

Lest it may be thought that Breslin's report is unduly severe, it is well to point out that it was presented, first to the Australian Prisoners' Rescue Committee and later to a convention of the Clan na Gael held in the following year. That convention approved it and ordered it printed for distribution to the branches. Tom Desmond, at that convention, fully endorsed Breslin's report and stated that he only signed the demand to be put ashore in order to prevent any serious trouble, owing to the feeling among the men. John King made a similar statement.

A special committee subsequently appointed by the Executive of Clan na Gael to investigate the *Catalpa* rescue censured Brennan and Duggan for their mischievous behaviour on the voyage home, and found that the causes of the *Catalpa* being brought to New York, instead of whaling as instructed, were the sickness of two of the prisoners, their fear of recapture, the dissatisfaction among them caused by some of the rescuers, the ill-feeling existing among the rescuers themselves and the note of protest which was presented to Breslin. (*Devoy's Post Bag*, I, 225-6).

The *Catalpa's* failure to remain out whaling caused much embarrassment to the Rescue Committee when it came to settlement with Captain Anthony and the other good Yankee friends whose help had made the expedition a success. Breslin and Anthony had certainly done their very best to carry out instructions, and it was no fault of theirs that the organisation was at a loss of thousands of dollars. One cannot but sympathise with Breslin. He had risked his life and liberty in freeing the men from captivity, and here they were, approaching New York harbour, their voyage completed and their liberty secure, with anything but a friendly regard towards their liberator. The *Catalpa* cast anchor in New York harbour about a mile from the Battery, at 2 a.m. on the morning of 19 August 1876. Breslin and Anthony had completed their mission with success and honour.

CHAPTER TWENTY-FIVE

GREETINGS AND CONTROVERSIES

ALTHOUGH it was well known that the *Catalpa* was on her way to America, her arrival in New York harbour was totally unexpected. No provision had been made for the men's reception. The Australian Rescue Committee had expected that they would be landed in Fernandina as arranged, and no one had even dreamed that they would want to be put ashore anywhere except the place appointed. The port collector of Fernandina would have notified New York of their arrival and this would have given the Clan time to prepare a full scale welcome. Besides, the Clan na Gael convention, which had figured in the discussion on board the *Catalpa,* was only just over, and many of the New York men who attended it had not yet come back to the city. A reception committee made up of men living in different cities had been appointed some time before, mainly to raise a fund for the benefit of the rescued men.

At daybreak John Breslin brought the news into the city. He went to O'Donovan Rossa's hotel at 182 Chatham Square and amongst the first who greeted him was William Foley, who had left Fremantle in January. Foley, already weak from heart disease, was so overcome with emotion on hearing the news that he fainted. Rossa was away in San Francisco. Devoy was laid up with a bad cold in Dr. Carroll's house in Philadelphia when he got a telegram from Denis, Rossa's eldest son, saying the *Catalpa* was in New York harbour. Devoy left his sick bed and took the next train to New York.

A party representing Clan na Gael set out from Rossa's to welcome the rescued men. They were placed in carriages and driven to the hotel, where hundreds had already gathered to greet them. Their reception is described by the *Irish World*:

> Rossa's hotel, on which the green flag was hoisted immediately on the arrival of the news, became the centre of attraction for nationalists. A constant stream of visitors kept pouring in throughout the day, and the "Catalpan Six" would have been quickly tired out but that the satisfaction at being freemen and compatriots did not allow any other feeling to affect them. They are all fine-looking men, Hogan, Darragh and Wilson in particular, and considering what they have come through in the last four months, they all look remarkably well. All were in the garb of sailors, provided them on board the *Catalpa.*—(Reprinted *United Irishman*—Liverpool—9 September 1876).

Devoy went to Rossa's hotel as soon as he reached New York. He had known all the men, except Darragh, since the time of his Fenian activities in Ireland. But he had known them as soldiers, disciplined, resolute and willing, and was not prepared for the change wrought on them by ten years of iron prison routine.

They welcomed him heartily, but almost at once their sense of grievance against Breslin broke out and Devoy was astonished to hear from them a volley of the most absurd complaints against the man who had risked life and liberty to free them. Put briefly, they considered that conditions on board the *Catalpa* did not measure up to the standards they would have liked, and they blamed Breslin for it. Devoy spoke to them in very plain language to disabuse them of this notion and his words had some effect on them, but he adds that he never "succeeded in removing the feeling of positive hatred, not to speak of ingratitude, which they entertained for Breslin." This, if true, makes sad reading, and one can only hope Devoy is overstating, but it was well that Breslin was not a hyper-sensitive man.

Unfortunately the rescued men soon after became implicated on one side or another in the clash which had already materialised between Devoy and the faction represented by John W. Goff. It would be tedious to go into this in detail. Enough to say that it culminated in the expulsion of Goff from the Clan na Gael organisation.

These things, however, were trifling compared with the mighty surge of exultation which was again renewed throughout the Irish world now that the men had safely landed. When it became known in New York that the rescued men were in Rossa's hotel, crowds gathered outside to greet, cheer and congratulate them. Other crowds rowed out into the harbour to see the rescue ship and its gallant captain. Messages of congratulation began to arrive from all sides. The extensive and lively Irish-American press applauded the deed, and the imagination and daring with which it was carried out.

The *Catalpa* remained only a short while in New York harbour. Whalers did not sojourn there and in any case New Bedford was the home port of ship and captain, so it continued its voyage, arriving at New Bedford city wharf on 24 August. That afternoon, when it was announced that the

Catalpa was coming into the harbour, great crowds assembled on the wharves to welcome home one of the bravest that ever lived of New Bedford's sons. An artillery salute of seventy-one cannon boomed out, one gun for every state in the Union and one for every county in Ireland. As soon as they landed, Captain Anthony, his officers and crew were invited to a public reception to be held the following day in Liberty Hall. At this reception Captain Anthony was the guest of honour. He is described in a contemporary account as short and slight of stature, with brown hair and eyes, straight, handsome features, square forehead, eyes deep-shrunken and dark, modest and retiring in demeanour and about thirty years of age. John Boyle O'Reilly was the orator on the occasion. After opening on a personal note in which he acknowledged his debt of gratitude to the faithful men of New Bedford who had rescued and befriended himself, he went on to pay a memorable tribute to the hero of the hour.

"We are here," he said, "to do honour and to show our gratitude to the man who has done a brave and wonderful deed. The self-sacrifice and unfailing devotion of him who took his life in his hand and beached his whaleboat on the penal colony, defying its fearful laws, defying the gallows and the chain-gang, in order to keep faith with the men who had placed their trust in him—this is almost beyond belief in our selfish and commonplace time." (*New Bedford Mercury*, reprinted in *The Irishman*, 16 September 1876).

O'Reilly also in his widely read *Pilot* recalled the rescue of Stephens in 1865. While the government was gloating over his capture, he vanished overnight from his prison cell as if by magic. It was cleverly, cleanly and bravely done without injury to anyone, without arrest, explanation or clue. The west Australian rescue resembled it in that it was done as daringly, silently and successfully. As in the case of Stephens, no trail remained, no price was paid in human life or anguish. Both rescues were cleanly accomplished from beginning to end, characteristic of the mind which planned them and the hands which brought them to a conclusion. In both, Breslin was the chief agent and Devoy his careful, patient planning fellow-worker. Men like these were not paid in words. They were of the mould that drew reward from the satisfaction of a deed well done.

Devoy considered that the major credit was Breslin's. There was glory enough in it for all concerned, he thought (*Gaelic American*, 2 July 1904), "but the man who won the victory in the crisis of the enterprise was John J. Breslin, and no decent Irishman will try to rob him of it." Michael Davitt thought likewise.

Dr. William Carroll, who was well qualified from his knowledge of the affair to say who deserved the main credit, gives it without reservation to John Devoy. Writing to Devoy on 8 June he states:

> Allow me to tender you my sincere congratulations on the successful termination of your years of labour and anxiety . . . Every one here [in Philadelphia] whom I have met, immediately on hearing it exclaimed (most naturally) "what a relief this will be to Devoy," and all proceeded to place the credit of the whole transaction where it belongs—to yourself . . . your work is done and well done.—(*Devoy's Post Bag*, I, 177).

We feel that every word of this tribute from Dr. Carroll to Devoy is fully deserved, just as we must endorse O'Reilly's judgment that no words can enhance the achievement of Devoy and Breslin in the matter. Yet we cannot help but feel that, if any one man emerged from the *Catalpa* expedition with something like heroic stature, that man is Captain George S. Anthony. Devoy, Breslin, Desmond, Talbot, O'Reilly and all the others who planned the rescue or took part in it were bound to the prisoners by ties of blood and brotherhood and revolution. It was their bounden duty to effect their release or at least to try. With Anthony it was different. No drop of Irish blood ran in his veins. He had no ties of brotherhood or nationality with the prisoners of Fremantle. There was every reason, apart from the risk, why he should not go at all on such a mission. Happily married, with an infant daughter, his prospects on shore or sea were bright and the men of the Clan na Gael were to him complete strangers. Yet go he did, and carried out his task with a spirit equal to anything in the records of chivalry. In taking six humble soldiers out of bondage into liberty he acted, as Boyle O'Reilly truly observed, in obedience to the law of God and humanity. Captain Anthony is the hero of the *Catalpa* expedition.

As for the police authorities at Perth, what could they deserve but our sincere sympathy? From beginning to end of the affair they were shadowed by some gremlin of misfortune, of Celtic provenance no doubt, which poked malicious fun at their earnest if not very inspired efforts to do something. The crowning act of irony perpetrated on itself under the influence of *gremlinus Celticus* by the Police Department of Perth took the form of the subjoined letter, which was addressed to:

The Officer in Charge of Police Department,
New Bedford,
Massachusetts,
United States America,

and reached its destination in August.

"The Officer in Charge of Police Department" at New Bedford was none other than Captain Henry Hathaway, City Marshal of New Bedford. No doubt he removed the cigar from his mouth to have a good laugh.

The letter is as follows:

Police Department,
Chief Office, Perth, Western Australia,
April 18, 1876.

Martin Hogan
Thomas Darragh
Robert Cranston
David or Michael } Harrington
Thomas Hassett
James Wilson

Sir:

I beg to inform you that on the 17th inst. the imperial convicts named in the margin absconded from the convict settlement at Fremantle in this colony, and escaped from the colony in the American whaling bark *Catalpa*, G. Anthony, master. This bark is from New Bedford, Massachusetts, U.S.A. The convicts were taken from the shore in a whale-boat belonging to the *Catalpa*, manned by Captain Anthony and six of the crew. The abettors were Collins, Jones and Johnson.

I attach a description of each of the absconders, and have to request that you will be good enough to furnish me with any particulars you may be able to gather concerning them.

I have the honour to be, sir, Your obedient servant,

M. A. Smith,
Supt. of Police.

To the Officer in charge of the Police Department,
New Bedford, Massachusetts, U.S.A.

Accompanying the letter was a copy of the *Police Gazette* of Western Australia containing a description of the men. This will be found in an appendix.

CHAPTER TWENTY-SIX

SETTLEMENT

THE rescued men had to be provided for in order to give them a fresh start in life. A new fund was opened for this purpose. Receptions were arranged for the men in various American cities and admission fees were charged. The men were divided up into twos or threes and sent to appear at these functions, which were largely attended and very successful. In this way about 15,000 dollars were collected and, after deduction of travelling expenses, divided between them.

There also remained the duty of settling with the captain and crew of the *Catalpa* and compensating them for the risk they had undertaken. Unforeseen difficulties made this a slow and tedious task. The gallant services of Captain Anthony to the Irish cause will be more fully appreciated when it is understood that they were given at the expense of his seafaring career. His action in taking his whaleboat to Rockingham beach and personally superintending the taking off of the men had made it impossible for him to enter a British port ever again. The ports throughout the world where whalers called to take supplies on board were largely in

British possession. The committee in charge of settlement were fully cognisant of the sacrifice entailed by his daring and selfless decision, as they were of the great services given to the Irish cause by Hathaway and Richardson. "We wanted," said Devoy, "to deal generously with all the men who had enabled us to carry out the rescue, to make a good impression that would be of service in future enterprises." Unfortunately, a small, ungracious knot of critics hampered the work of this committee by insisting on making what they called a "good business" bargain with the three men who had assisted them so generously. The result was that their Yankee friends received less remuneration than their great services deserved. Many journeys had to be made to New Bedford to discuss details of the settlement, which was finally effected, in February 1877, by a three-man committee consisting of Devoy, Breslin and William Cannon.

They settled with Richardson, Anthony and Hathaway on the following basis. They took the *Whaleman's Shipping List*, made an average of the catch taken by all the other whalers which sailed out of New Bedford during April 1875, and of the prices received for the oil, and assumed that the *Catalpa* had made that average. Each man's "lay," or share, from the captain's down, was calculated at that average, and the men were duly paid off. The ship was then valued at $6,000 and made over to Richardson to conclude the settlement with himself, Anthony and Hathaway. Devoy learned afterwards that the price realised by the sale of the ship fell short of this figure, so that Richardson, Anthony and Hathaway fared worse than is indicated in the financial report printed at the end of this book. On the whole, Devoy was not particularly happy about the settlement. In the case of Anthony, specifically, he considered that it was made on a very illiberal basis and that he was only given just a little more than he would have earned on an average whaling cruise of the same length of time. But Anthony never grumbled and never regretted what he had done. He was always proud, and justly so, of his work and always grateful for Irish acknowledgment of it. The Executive of Clan na Gael voted Breslin and Desmond

$1,000 each and King $500. The entire cost of the expedition came to nearly $26,000

The rescued men settled down in America and became integrated into its life, environment and pursuits. Before the year was out Cranston married. He became a staunch supporter of O'Donovan Rossa. They all pursued their various avocations in a freedom they had never before known. The years passed and the identity given them by their great adventure became dimmed by the obscuring hand of time. When Eamon de Valera as President of the Irish Republic toured the States in 1920 there was one man still surviving of that little band of rescued men. He was the man who had sent the appeal, like a voice from the tomb, out of Fremantle prison, James Wilson, and he, long a citizen of the American Republic, conversed with the President of the emergent Irish Republic about his escape, about his friend O'Donovan Rossa and about his hopes for Ireland's destiny. He had lived to see great changes, greatest of all for him the proclamation in arms of the Republic which he, half a century before, had taken the oath of a soldier of liberty to accomplish.

John Breslin became prominent in the Clan na Gael organisation for his ability and practical turn of mind. As a trustee of O'Donovan Rossa's famous Skirmishing Fund he became involved in many hectic controversies. He superintended the construction and trials of the *Fenian Ram*, the first submarine ever built, the designer of which was Clareman John P. Holland, and the purpose of which was to carry out undersea attacks on British naval units. He became John Devoy's assistant in the management of the *Irish Nation* weekly, and enriched Irish-American historical literature by his remarkable letter in reply to a New York committee which invited him to a meeting expressing disapproval of the assassination of Burke and Cavendish in the Phoenix Park. His early death in 1887 was a serious loss to Clan na Gael.

James Reynolds, who was born in Moynah in the parish of Drumlumman, County Cavan, was 45 years old at the time of the rescue. Later, during some of the most strenuous years of Clan na Gael history, he occupied a position on the Executive Body and became involved in the great controversies which rocked the organisation. In New Haven, where he was respected by all, he received many civic honours in his lifetime. Enough of private sorrow came his way. Four of his five children died in his lifetime; the fifth survived him only a short while. He died in New Haven in August 1897. When, in July 1904, a fine celtic cross was unveiled over his grave in St. Lawrence cemetery, a host of former friends, including Devoy and Goff, turned up to do honour to the memory of Catalpa Jim, and ex-Congressman Piggott retold the great story at his graveside.

Peter Curran, the accidental discovery of whose address led to the adventure, died in New York on 30 December 1881, and is buried in Calvary cemetery.

Captain Anthony had perforce to retire from the sea. He spent the remainder of his life in New Bedford, where he obtained a position at a modest salary in the custom house. This he held up till the time of his death. In 1897 he published his personal account of the voyage and rescue, *The Catalpa Expedition*. In the writing of this he had the assistance of a young journalist friend, Zephaniah Pease. Between them they produced one of the most unique books in the annals of seafaring, which has now become so rare as to be much prized by collectors. Captain Anthony died at the age of seventy, on 22 May 1913. To the end of his life he remained poor in the world's goods, but in character, courage and integrity few men have been so rarely endowed. He was a typical old-time American gentleman. His wife and daughter survived him. In the year 1920, when the President of the Irish Republic, Eamon de Valera, was touring the States, one of the highlights of his itinerary was his visit to New Bedford. At Fall River he met Captain Henry Hathaway, then as always an enthusiastic supporter of the Irish battle for freedom, and at New Bedford the President, accompanied by Captain Anthony's wife and daughter, placed the colours of the Irish Republic on Captain Anthony's grave, as a tribute of affection and respect on behalf of the Irish nation to which, many years before, Captain Anthony had rendered such memorable service.

Captain Anthony's deed is his enduring testament. His name will never be forgotten in Ireland and his memory will always be venerated by Irishmen along with the great heroes of their own race.

CHAPTER TWENTY-SEVEN

EPILOGUE:

CLAN NA GAEL AND JOHN DEVOY

THERE was one essential step which the rescue indicated must be taken at once. A closer union between the Clan na Gael and the home organisation was imperative. An I.R.B. envoy had visited the States in 1874 and since, in his capacity, he had a right to the information, he was told about the rescue plans. Before leaving America, however, he publicly took up an attitude at variance with Clan na Gael policy. When he returned to Ireland he kept the knowledge of the American rescue preparations to himself. On the other hand, he encouraged in every way the organisation of an independent I.R.B. rescue effort, which was begun as a result of appeals sent by Martin Hogan to his family in Limerick. The knowledge of this was also concealed by the envoy from the American organisation, so that preparations for the same end were being made on both sides of the Atlantic with each side unaware of what the other was doing. It was only by a stroke of good fortune that things developed so as to bring about a fusion of forces between the two sets of agents in Fremantle. A closer union was therefore indicated and consequently brought about, with a united policy, as outlined in the amended Clan constitution of 1877.

The *Catalpa* rescue gave the morale of the Clan, and of Irish-America in general, a mighty uplift. It showed what could be done by a united, disciplined and resolute organisation. Thereafter Clan na Gael extended its sinews from New

York westwards to 'Frisco, northwards to Boston and points beyond, and southwards to New Orleans, until camps flourished in every territory, state and city of the American Union. It became the inspiration and the great unseen driving force behind the combination of the Land League and Parnellite movements, which were organised on a vast scale in America as auxiliaries of the movement in Ireland. The hard resolute sinews of the organisation extended wherever the Irish had settled in the United States, and caused revolutionary activity to flourish in hundreds of centres.

There were eminent men in the Irish National movement in America who were not members of the Clan, John Boyle O'Reilly for example, Patrick Collins and Patrick Ford. These were men who had achieved eminence by virtue of their own individual merit and capacity. Membership of the Clan might not harmonise with the position O'Reilly occupied as editor of the Boston *Pilot*, one of the great Catholic weeklies of America. In fact, his Archbishop had asked him to resign his membership, but he continued to be consulted by the Clan on all important questions of policy. Although the membership of the Clan was predominantly Catholic, it was generally understood that the Church withheld favour from organisations which operated in secrecy. Yet so legitimate were the political aims of the Clan held to be in republican America that no clash occurred, and the censure of Dr. Bernard McQuade, Bishop of Rochester, was more than offset by the memorable declaration in favour of Irish national aspirations by Bishop Gilmour of Cleveland, a declaration which justified the aims of Clan na Gael and was given its due prominence in the columns of the *Irish Nation* by John Devoy.

There were other men who were expelled from the Clan. These included the indomitable fighter, O'Donovan Rossa. Certain rules of the Clan were meant to be obeyed or expulsion was the penalty. These were no toleration of "kickers." But it was easier to bridle the lion than to hold to rule the obstinate, rugged, magnificent individualism of Rossa.

When speaking of Clan na Gael we naturally think of John Devoy. For Devoy more than anyone else was the maker of the Clan and the greatest influence in its history. He it was primarily who moulded and fashioned it. He was the master, the disciplinarian, the man of authority. Men like that do not fail to make enemies and the list of enemies incurred by John Devoy is a terrifying one. John W. Goff, Rossa, Patrick Egan, Patrick Ford, Michael Kerwin, Alec Sullivan, Joe McGarrity, to name only a few. Not to mention men from outside the States from Michael Davitt to Eamon de Valera.

Part of the trouble sprang from the fact that Devoy refused to countenance any other Irish revolutionary organisation in America except Clan na Gael. He believed that the Clan, because of its history and experience, had assumed the right to control all revolutionary activity and he would tolerate no factions. On the other hand, Patrick Ford, a man of considerable influence, held the view that the best results would be obtained by different organisations, each working towards Irish independence by its own methods, competing with each other, but not clashing with one another. Devoy and Ford would not agree on a lonely desert island.

The Clan was in the full tide of its strength between 1880 and 1886, shoulder to shoulder with Parnell, independent of British retaliation, a vast and powerful Irish dominion within a dominion. Its strength was shattered because there are no bounds to the ambition of men. In this case the high ambition of Alexander Sullivan was the evil cause of splitting the Clan into two warring factions. It is admitted on all sides that Sullivan was one of the most talented men in the annals of the Irish-American movement. It is hard to say how much of his success and ambition he owed his wife, formerly Margaret Buchanan, for she was a lady of talent and high spirit herself. Sullivan possessed the temper of steel. He had killed a man for an alleged insult to his wife.

John Devoy met a redoubtable foe in the person of Alec Sullivan. Sullivan did his utmost to use his position in Clan na Gael and avail of the Clan machinery in order to rise to power in American politics. In 1884 he manoeuvred skilfully to obtain the Democratic nomination for the American vice-presidency and tried to obtain Clan support to that end, but a word from Devoy shattered his ambitious plan. For it was clear to Devoy that the ambitions of Alec Sullivan would weaken the Clan in its capacity to serve Ireland. Sullivan thought otherwise. "You are not," said Devoy, "American-born and so are ineligible." Sullivan neither forgave nor forgot. From 1884 on the friction between them increased, and the unity of the Clan na Gael began to be seriously impaired.

About this time Sullivan and his two allies, Mike Boland and Denis Feely, by irregular methods, obtained control of the administrative machinery of Clan na Gael. These three became known as "The Triangle" and acquired dictatorial authority over the organisation, but the guiding genius was Alec Sullivan. Sullivan played havoc with Clan policy. He severed connections with the I.R.B. and authorised retaliatory action by dynamite on England in the course of which William Lomasney was killed and many others arrested. He is also alleged on reliable evidence to have misappropriated a large amount of Clan funds with which he gambled on the Chicago Stock Exchange.

Devoy changed his residence from New York to Chicago to keep a closer watch on Sullivan's irregular activities. There was a tense moment one day when they met face to face in a Chicago restaurant. Well aware that Sullivan's cool, deliberate mind might at any moment order the death of his opponent, Devoy kept his hand on his revolver until they got out of sight of each other. The rift in the Clan was revealed to the whole world in 1889 when Dr. Patrick Cronin of Chicago, a strong critic of Alec Sullivan's, was found brutally murdered. In the sensational trial which followed, four men were sentenced to long terms of imprisonment, and the intimate affairs of the Clan were broadcast throughout the States. The organisation was publicly split from coast to coast, and loud was the clamour of the American tories calling for its suppression.

It took eleven years to heal the terrible wounds. Long

conferences were held in 1899 with a view to effecting union, the way being made easier by the retirement from Clan affairs of Alec Sullivan. In these conferences Devoy took a leading and constructive part. The final meeting of reconciliation took place in Dooner's Hotel, Philadelphia, on 5 September 1899, and the first convention of the reunited Clan took place in Atlantic City in 1900.

Thereafter John Devoy became the acknowledged authority in Clan na Gael. He kneaded the Clan into a superb fighting organisation which gave essential support to the Gaelic League, Sinn Fein and the I.R.B. The financial assistance sent by the Clan to Ireland helped the forces of revolution to strike their historic blow in Easter Week. Of that fact John Devoy felt justly proud.

The rule and authority which he had exercised in the affairs of the Clan for forty years gave John Devoy a claim on the hegemony and direction of the organisation, which he operated with some suspicion against outsiders and "butters-in." America was Clan territory, and it was understood and accepted by Irish leaders, like Parnell and Davitt, that the rulers of Irish-America, and they only, held authority in that sphere. John Devoy had written in 1882:

> The Irish people at home decide their own policy, and we in this country simply follow and sustain them, but our own internal government and the decision of the measures necessary for the fulfilmen of the home policy are matters for our own consideration.

This was crystal clear, and any appeals to Irish-Amer which did not take it into consideration were bound to re in disaster. Disregard of this established policy lay at root of the devastating cleavage of 1919-20. The Clan n recovered from the split of 1920. After the establishme Saorstát Éireann its capacity to render service to Ireland less and less, and the death of Devoy in 1928 remove greatest leader Irish-America had ever known.

Looking back on the history and achievements of C Gael, what can be said other than that it was a mag organisation. Great men had taken part in its affa above and beyond everything else, John Devoy wa helm. Many indeed were Devoy's faults. An authoritarian, with a fierce power of invective, suspicious, strong in his own opinion, impatient of another's opinion. His enemies used to say he was dour, sullen, distant, with a scowl on his countenance and a frown on his forehead.

Let them say. When all is said and done, the verdict of Patrick Pearse on John Devoy stands true and incontrovertible, that John Devoy was the greatest hero of the Fenian host. Devoy was the general, the strategist and the planning genius. John Devoy was Clan na Gael, and Clan na Gael was John Devoy.

Many was the occasion during his long career of service in the cause of Ireland that *The Times* cast a cold eye on the activities which were encouraged by John Devoy. The cause for which he strove, however, went a long way towards success in his lifetime and with this measure of success came a more sober appraisal of his qualities from unexpected quarters. His obituary in *The Times* (of 1 October 1928) is grave and respectful. It says:

> Mr. John Devoy . . . was the oldest of Irish revolutionaries and
> most bitter and persistent, as well as the most dangerous enemy
> his country Ireland has produced since Wolfe Tone, the organiser
> United Irish movement at the end of the 18th century, brought
> the attempted invasion of Ireland by the French under Hoche.
> ty years Devoy was unremittingly engaged in conspiracies,
> Ireland and in America, for the establishment of an Irish
> c.

was a fine tribute.

APPENDIX I.

Description of the escaped men from the *Police Gazette* of Western Australia. *The Irishman,* 26 August 1876 (reprinted from Boston *Pilot*):

> Thomas Darragh, Imperial Convict, Reg. No. 9707; arrived in the Colony per convict ship *Hougoumont,* 10th January 1868; sentenced for life, 2nd March, 1866. Description—Stout, age 42 years, height 5 feet 6½ inches, red hair, grey eyes, round visage, fresh complexion. Marks—Mole on right cheek; mole on breast; is much freckled; square shoulders, and walks erect. Fenian. Absconded from Fremantle 8.30 a.m. 17th April, 1876.
>
> Martin Hogan, Imperial Convict, Reg. No. 9767; arrived in the Colony per convict ship *Hougoumont*; received a life sentence, 21st August, 1866. Description—Stout, age 37 years, height 5 feet 6 inches, dark brown hair, dark hazel eyes, long visage, dark complexion. Marks—D left side; cut left eyebrow, walks firmly; has the gait and appearance of a cavalry soldier; is a coachpainter; Fenian. Absconded from Fremantle 8.30 a.m., 17th April, 1876.
>
> Michael Harrington, Imperial Convict, Reg. No. 9757; arrived in the Colony per convict ship *Hougoumont*; received life sentence, July 7, 1866. Description—Middling stout, age 48 years, 5 feet 7½ inches high, brown hair, grey eyes, full visage, sallow complexion. Marks—D left side; pockmarked. Fenian. Absconded at 8.30 a.m. from Fremantle, on 17th April, 1876.
>
> Thomas Hassett, Imperial Convict, Reg. No. 9758; arrived in the Colony per convict ship *Hougoumont*; received life sentence, 15th August, 1866. Description—Middling stout, age 36 years, height 5 feet 8 inches, brown hair, light grey eyes, long visage, fresh complexion. Marks—D left side; cut mark left side upper lip; a rough carpenter. Fenian.
>
> Robert Cranston, Imperial Convict, Reg. No. 9702; arrived in the Colony per convict ship *Hougoumont,* 1868; received life sentence 26th June, 1866. Description—Middling stout, age 36 years, height 5 feet 6¾ inches, brown hair, grey eyes, oval visage, fresh complexion. Marks—Cross inside right arm, a farmer. Fenian. Absconded at 8.30 a.m. from Fremantle on 17th April.
>
> James Wilson, Imperial Convict, Reg. No. 9915; arrived in the Colony per convict ship *Hougoumont*; received life sentence, 20th August, 1866. Description—Middling stout, age 40 years, height 5 feet 8¼ inches, brown hair, grey eyes, oval visage, fresh complexion. Marks—D left side; is a labourer.

APPENDIX II.

(From the *Gaelic American* 1 October 1904)

FINANCES OF THE *CATALPA*

(Abstract)

STATEMENT OF THE AUSTRALIAN PRISONERS RESCUE FUND

RECEIPTS

Per Treasurer's report July 15, 1875, as follows:

From District	$8,473.69	
" "	1,759.17	
" "	880.00	
" "	1,556.00	
" "	404.00	
" "	7,065.63	
" "	50.00	
		20,188.49
Error in above		10.00

Per Treasurer's report, August 8, 1876, as follows:

From District	$516.00	
" "	370.25	
" "	200.00	
" "	199.60	
" "	500.00	
Interest	42.48	
		1,828.33

J. T. Richardson, agent for oil $3,000, less interest (Report $4,794.68 and interest $43.17 equal to $4,838.15, less on hand $53.99 equal to $4,784.16).	2,955.83
To cash, gold received in California by J. J. Breslin	1,200.00
To cash, gold received in Sydney by J. J. Breslin	850.00
To cash, gold received from Sydney by J. J. Breslin, £384	1,920.00
To profit of voyage, by J. T. Richardson . .	2,391.00
To cash allowed for *Catalpa*	6,000.00
To interest, per Treasurer	180.06
	$37,523.71

DISBURSEMENTS

By cost and outfit of *Catalpa* and advances to crew		$18,914.82
By expended through J. W. Goff . . .		372.53
By expended through J. Devoy		289.57
By expenses of J. J. Breslin, as follows:		
Paid him by Goff . . .	$118.48	
Paid him by Treasurer . . .	400.00	
Paid him by Treasurer . . .	600.00	
Paid him by Treasurer . . .	407.35	
Paid him by Sheares Club . .	1,000.00	
Expenses of Breslin besides above advances	824.95	
		3,350.78
By expenses of T. Desmond		1,000.00
By expenses of J. Reynolds		35.00
By transfer to general fund		14.65
By expense of Treasurer to New Bedford . .		30.46
By expense, Garaghy family		69.10
By D. Duggan, account of family . . .		35.00
By telegrams, etc., Devoy		8.50
By Thomas Brennan, per Goff		125.00
By expense of Reynolds to New Bedford . .		56.66
By expense of Devoy to New Bedford . .		29.80
By D. Duggan, per A		40.00
By Smith, per A		5.00
By John King		500.00
By J. J. Breslin		1,000.00
By J. T. Richardson, outlay		3,044.40
By J. T. Richardson, advanced to Committee, and interest		3,142.50
By H. C. Hathaway		1,000.00
By Captain Anthony		1,000.00
By S. P. Smith		200.00
By Balance on hand		3,260.54
		$37,524.31
Net cost of the enterprise to the Committee . .		26,070.47
Less $208.25 and $4.20		212.45
		$25,858.02

Amount paid Captain Anthony:

Share of voyage as per average . . .	$2,165.63
Gratuity for rescue	1,000.00
Total . .	$3,165.63

Amount paid Mate, S. P. Smith:

Share of voyage as per average . . .	$1,443.75
Gratuity for rescue	200.00
Total . .	$1,643.75

BIBLIOGRAPHY

MSS

Fenian Papers in the State Paper Office, Dublin Castle.

NEWSPAPERS AND JOURNALS.

AMERICAN:

The Gaelic American (New York)

This weekly, of which John Devoy was editor, is the most important source of information about the *Catalpa* expedition. Between 16 July and 22 October 1904, it gives Devoy's detailed account, the portions of John J. Breslin's report describing his sojourn in Western Australia, the actual rescue and the return voyage, and John King's personal narrative. Additional details are given in other issues, e.g. 9 July 1904, 31 May 1913, 22 November 1924. John J. Breslin's report was first published in the *New York Herald* from which it was copied into other papers.

The Irish World (New York)

Thomas Darragh's account of the escape is given in the issue of 26 August 1876.

The United Irishman (New York)
The Irish Nation (New York)
The Irish Republic (Chicago and New York)

IRISH:

The Irishman (Dublin)

A very important source for Fenian history.

The Irish People (Dublin, 1899, 1900)

Editor, William O'Brien, M.P. Contains a valuable series *The Dawn of Fenianism* by James J. O'Kelly, M.P., beginning 16 September 1899.

Irish Freedom (Dublin)
The United Irishman (Dublin)
Editor, Arthur Griffith.

BRITISH:

The United Irishman (Liverpool)

Organ of the Home Rule Confederation of Great Britain. Editor, John Denvir. This weekly contains details I have not seen elsewhere, e.g. Fremantle prison regulations, 17 June 1876, etc. The editor was connected with the independent I.R.B. rescue scheme and was personally acquainted with John Walsh. John J. Breslin, through his brother Michael, sent him directly a copy of his report, which is printed extensively in the issue of 9 September 1876. It differs slightly in certain details from that in the *Gaelic American*.

The Times

OFFICIAL PUBLICATIONS, REPORTS, ETC.

Hansard: Commons Debate of 22 May 1876. Vol. CCXXIX, col. 1040-52.

The Special Commission Act, 1888. *Report of Proceedings, Times* reprint. 4 vols., London, 1890 (*The Times*).

Report of the Proceedings of the Special Commission for the trial of Thomas Clarke Luby and Others for Treason-Felony, Dublin 1866 (Alexander Thom).

County Kerry Summer Assizes, 1867, in *Reports of Proceedings at the Special Commissions* (1867), etc., Dublin 1871 (Alexander Thom).

BOOKS AND PAMPHLETS.

O'Brien, William and Ryan, Desmond, Editors: *Devoy's Post Bag*, 2 Vols., Dublin 1948 and 1953 (Fallon).

Cleary, P. S.: *Australia's Debt to Irish Nation Builders*, Sydney 1933 (Angus and Robertson).

Crowley, F. K.: *Australia's Western Third*, London 1960 (Macmillan).

Davitt, Michael: *Life and Progress in Australasia*, London 1898 (Methuen).

Denvir, John: *The Life Story of an Old Rebel*, Dublin 1910 (Sealy, Bryers and Walker).

The Catalpa: the story of the rescue of the military Fenians, Liverpool n.d. (Denvir).

Devoy, John: *Recollections of an Irish Rebel*, New York 1928 (Charles D. Young).

Doheny, Michael: *The Felon's Track*, Dublin 1914 (Gill).

King, Clyde L.: *The Fenian Movement* in *University of Colorado Studies* April 1909, pp. 187-213, Boulder, Colo.

McEnnis, John T.: *Clan na Gael and the Murder of Dr. Cronin*, Chicago 1889 (n.p.).

Mann, Arthur: *Yankee Reformers in the Urban Age*, Belknap Press of Harvard Univ. Press, Cambridge, Mass., 1954.

O'Connor, T. P., and McWade, R.: *Parnell, Gladstone and the Great Irish Struggle*, New York 1886 (C. V. LeCraw).

O'Donnell, Frank Hugh: *A History of the Irish Parliamentary Party*, 2 Vols., London 1910 (Longmans Green).

O'Donovan Rossa: *Irish Rebels in English Prisons: A Record of Prison Life*, New York 1882 (P. J. Kenedy).

O'Leary, John: *Recollections of Fenians and Fenianism*, 2 Vols., London 1896 (Downey).

Pease, Zephaniah W.: *The Catalpa Expedition*, New Bedford, Mass. 1897 (George S. Anthony).

Reid, Sir Thomas Wemyss: *The Life of the Right Honourable William Edward Forster*, 2 Vols., London 1888 (Chapman and Hall).

Roche, James J.: *Life of John Boyle O'Reilly*, New York 1891 (Cassell).

Ryan, Dr. Mark: *Fenian Memories*, Dublin 1946 (Gill).

Schofield, William G.: *Seek for a Hero*, New York 1956 (Kenedy).

Tynan, P. J. P.: *The Irish National Invincibles and their Times*, London 1894 (Chatham).

The Rescue of the Military Fenians from Australia with a memoir of John Devoy, Dublin 1929 (Nugent and Co.).

WORKS OF REFERENCE.

Annual Register

The Australian Encyclopaedia (1958)

Dictionary of American Biography

Dictionary of National Biography

Thom's Directory

An Anvil Book

The Mystery of the Casement Ship

By CAPTAIN KARL SPINDLER

'The Casement Ship' had many names. Originally, the *Castro*, owned by the Wilson Line of Hull, she had been brought in as a prize by a German destroyer in the early days of the first world war. As the *Libau* she sailed from Lubeck, on April 9, 1916, on the 'special expedition,' with a cargo of obsolete Russian rifles, ten modern machine-guns, ammunition and explosives—the German contribution to the Irish rising of 1916. Her destination was Tralee bay. After she sailed, her commander, Karl Spindler, a lieutenant in the Imperial German naval reserve, changed her name yet once more, and as the *Aud*, a neutral Norwegian, she masqueraded during her exciting few remaining days.

This account of the voyage is a narrative of almost incredible daring, hazard and near-success. The *Aud* steamed up the west coast of Norway, far north, and then down the Atlantic, around the north of Scotland. Off Rockall, she survived the worst storm in the experience of her captain. She played a game of blind-man's-buff with the British patrols, was scrutinised twice but not stopped. Spindler seemed indeed a child of good fortune. Astonishingly, he had taken his ship through the British naval blockade. She cast anchor at the appointed place, off Inishtooskert, in Tralee bay, at 4.15 p.m. on Holy Thursday, April 20. Then Spindler's good fortune deserted him. Towards 6 p.m. on Good Friday, April 21, he was caught in a net of British ships, which extended from the Fastnet to Loop Head. He had no choice but to accompany a number of them to Queenstown harbour for examination. At the harbour mouth he blew up his ship. Spindler and his men were soon bound for prisoner-of-war camps in England, and he was to make a sensational escape bid from one of them.

In a valuable foreword to this edition, Florence O'Donoghue presents a new and impartial study of the attempt to land the arms from Germany, based in part on materials not hitherto available. He gives an illuminating interpretation of the events connected with the negotiations for the importation of arms, and the reasons for the failure of the enterprise.

PAPER-BACK EDITION 3/6